"Christmas—it's the most wonderful time of the year, except… it's full of busyness and the stress of the season! So Tim Chester provides some timely soul nourishment with this Advent devotional around Luke's four Christmas canticles. He writes in a way that brings back 'the wonder'. Read it and let your heart sing!"

STEVE JAMES, Former Rector, Holy Trinity Platt, Manchester; Chair of Langham Arts

"In *With Heart and Soul and Voice*, Tim Chester unpacks the history, heart and hope behind the four songs surrounding Christ's birth. With skill, creativity and insight, he helps us to see with fresh eyes the depths of our sin and the heights of God's mercy revealed in Jesus coming to die for our sins. If you're looking for an Advent devotional that makes you want to sing, look no further!"

BOB KAUFLIN, Director, Sovereign Grace Music

"Tim Chester's *With Heart and Soul and Voice* invites us to hear the songs of the first Christmas with fresh ears. Rooted in Luke's Gospel, this Advent devotional draws us into the deeper story behind the Nativity—so that our hearts might sing with renewed hope and great joy."

MATT BOSWELL, Hymn-writer; Pastor, The Trails Church, Celina, Texas; Professor of Worship Ministries, Midwestern Baptist Theological Seminary

"So much of the story, the joy and the courage we need each day is carried in the songs of the Bible. Tim Chester helps us savor these life-giving lyrics."

KRISTYN GETTY, Hymn-writer;
Co-Founder, Getty Music

"In 24 short reflections, Tim Chester leads us through Luke's Nativity songs. We listen to 'the soundtrack of the first Christmas' with a new delight. We share the excitement of the singers of these songs as they realise that the treasured hopes of God's people are met in the Christ child. This book is inspiring and heart-warming. It is highly recommended."

PAUL MALLARD, Director for the West Midlands and
Chair of Theology Team, FIEC

WITH HEART & SOUL & VOICE

With Heart and Soul and Voice

© Tim Chester, 2025

Published by:
The Good Book Company

thegoodbook.com | thegoodbook.co.uk
thegoodbook.com.au | thegoodbook.co.nz

Unless indicated, all Scripture references are taken from the Holy Bible, New International Version. Copyright © 2011 Biblica. Used by permission. Emphasis added is the author's own.

English translations of *Magnificat, Benedictus, Gloria in Excelsis* and *Nunc Dimittis* © 1998 English Language Liturgical Consultation (ELLC), and used by permission. www.englishtexts.org.

All rights reserved. Except as may be permitted by the Copyright Act, no part of this publication may be reproduced in any form or by any means without prior permission from the publisher.

Tim Chester has asserted his right under the Copyright, Designs and Patents Act 1988 to be identified as author of this work.

Cover design by Studio Gearbox | Design and art direction by André Parker

ISBN: 9781802543223 | JOB-008185 | Printed in India

Contents

Introduction	9
Mary's Song: The Magnificat	13
1. Noticed	17
2. Reversed	23
3. Lifted	27
4. Beginnings	31
5. Servant	35
6. Temple	39
7. Mercy	43
Zechariah's Song: The Benedictus	49
8. Prophecy	55
9. Coming	61
10. Promised	67
11. Freedom	73
12. Forgiveness	77

13. Dawn	81
14. Praise	85
The Angels' Song: The Gloria	89
15. Peace	91
16. War	95
17. Seated	99
18. Power	103
19. Glory	107
Simeon's Song: The Nunc Dimittis	111
20. Waiting	113
21. Sleeping	119
22. Prepared	125
23. Exposed	129
24. Rewarded	133
Endnotes	139

Introduction

Sometimes I wander into our living room and start watching the TV drama that my wife's already watching. After a few minutes my wife turns to me and asks me a question about what's going on. "How should I know?" I protest. "You're the one watching it. You tell me!"

It's a bit like this with the Christmas story—we've wandered into the drama halfway through. It's not difficult to work out that a child is being born, but we don't know why this might be important. Why are people responding in the way they do? Are we supposed to be happy or sad? What exactly is going on? Fortunately, the Gospel writer Luke is a bit more sympathetic than I am; he fills us in on the story so far.

In the olden days—back before we all binge-watched box sets on Netflix—you had to wait a week between episodes in a TV series. The problem was that by the time the next episode rolled round, you couldn't remember all the twists and turns from the previous week. So programme makers often included a short montage of clips from previous episodes to remind you of what had come before. Luke does something very much like this at the start of his Gospel.

Luke's Christmas story is the beginning of his presentation of Jesus. But the story of Jesus is in fact the climax of a centuries-long story. You can kind of make sense of Jesus just by reading an account of his life, but if you really want to understand who he is and what he came to do, then you need to know something about what came before. You need to know *the story so far*. Professor Robert Tannehill says, "We cannot understand what the excitement is about unless we realise that ancient hopes, treasured in the hearts of the Jewish people, are coming to fulfilment … The Gospel of Luke begins in mid-story and immediately makes us aware of that fact."[1]

The main way that Luke catches us up is by including four songs in his account of the Nativity—the songs of Mary, Zechariah, the angels and Simeon. These songs provide the soundtrack to the first Christmas. Each one is Luke's equivalent of a montage of previous highlights. They orient us to what's happening in this, the denouement of the drama. So you could think of this book as the programme notes for the musical performance that unfolds in Luke's Christmas story.

It's also significant that Luke chooses to catch us up through songs. There are several other ways in which he could have done it. Matthew does it by quoting from the Old Testament and telling us how these patterns and promises are being fulfilled in the birth of Jesus. John skips the Christmas story altogether and in its place gives us a rich reflection on the Word made flesh. Two good options. But Luke does something different: he curates the first Christmas carol concert.

Luke wants to make our hearts sing. What's happening in Bethlehem is so amazing that it needs to be accompanied by worship. Luke is putting words in our mouths so that we can join the celebration.

My interest in these songs arose because I follow the Divine Office—the pattern of daily liturgy used by the church over the centuries. This means that I recite Zechariah's song each morning when I say Morning Prayer, Mary's song in Evening Prayer, and often Simeon's song in Compline or Night Prayer. The liturgical forms of these songs are commonly known by their opening words in Latin; Mary's song is the *Magnificat*, Zechariah's song is the *Benedictus*, Simeon's is the *Nunc Dimittis*, and *Gloria in Excelsis* is an expanded form of the angels' song. This daily repetition forces you to think hard about the words of each song and how to make them your own. This book arises out of this spiritual routine and my attempts to engage fully with the message of these songs, day by day. As you approach Christmas, my prayer is that they will make your heart sing.

Mary's Song:
The Magnificat

My soul proclaims the greatness of the Lord,
my spirit rejoices in God my Saviour;
he has looked with favour on his lowly servant.

From this day all generations will call me blessed;
the Almighty has done great things for me
and holy is his name.

He has mercy on those who fear him,
from generation to generation.

He has shown strength with his arm
and has scattered the proud in their conceit,

Casting down the mighty from their thrones
and lifting up the lowly.

He has filled the hungry with good things
and sent the rich away empty.

He has come to the aid of his servant Israel,
to remember his promise of mercy,

The promise made to our ancestors,
to Abraham and his children for ever.

Luke 1:26-55

²⁶ In the sixth month of Elizabeth's pregnancy, God sent the angel Gabriel to Nazareth, a town in Galilee, ²⁷ to a virgin pledged to be married to a man named Joseph, a descendant of David. The virgin's name was Mary. ²⁸ The angel went to her and said, "Greetings, you who are highly favoured! The Lord is with you."

²⁹ Mary was greatly troubled at his words and wondered what kind of greeting this might be. ³⁰ But the angel said to her, "Do not be afraid, Mary, you have found favour with God. ³¹ You will conceive and give birth to a son, and you are to call him Jesus. ³² He will be great and will be called the Son of the Most High. The Lord God will give him the throne of his father David, ³³ and he will reign over Jacob's descendants for ever; his kingdom will never end."

³⁴ "How will this be," Mary asked the angel, "since I am a virgin?"

³⁵ The angel answered, "The Holy Spirit will come on you, and the power of the Most High will overshadow you. So the holy one to be born will be called the Son of God. ³⁶ Even Elizabeth your relative is going to have a child in her old age, and she who was said to be unable to conceive is in her sixth month. ³⁷ For no word from God will ever fail."

³⁸ "I am the Lord's servant," Mary answered. "May your word to me be fulfilled." Then the angel left her.

³⁹ At that time Mary got ready and hurried to a town in the hill country of Judea, ⁴⁰ where she entered Zechariah's home and greeted Elizabeth. ⁴¹ When Elizabeth heard Mary's greeting, the baby leaped in her womb, and Elizabeth was filled with the Holy Spirit. ⁴² In a loud voice she exclaimed: "Blessed are you among women, and blessed is the child you will bear! ⁴³ But why am I so favoured, that the mother of my Lord should come to me? ⁴⁴ As soon as the sound of your greeting reached my ears, the baby in my womb leaped for joy. ⁴⁵ Blessed is she who has believed that the Lord would fulfil his promises to her!"

⁴⁶ And Mary said:
"My soul glorifies the Lord
 ⁴⁷ and my spirit rejoices in God my Saviour,
⁴⁸ for he has been mindful
 of the humble state of his servant.
From now on all generations will call me blessed,
 ⁴⁹ for the Mighty One has done great things for me—
holy is his name.
⁵⁰ His mercy extends to those who fear him,
 from generation to generation.
⁵¹ He has performed mighty deeds with his arm;
 he has scattered those who are proud in their
  inmost thoughts.
⁵² He has brought down rulers from their thrones
 but has lifted up the humble.
⁵³ He has filled the hungry with good things
 but has sent the rich away empty.
⁵⁴ He has helped his servant Israel,
 remembering to be merciful
⁵⁵ to Abraham and his descendants for ever,
 just as he promised our ancestors."

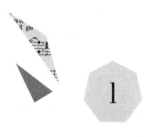

1

Noticed

Magnificat

My soul proclaims the greatness of the Lord,
  my spirit rejoices in God my Saviour;
he has looked with favour on his lowly servant.

From this day all generations will call me blessed;
the Almighty has done great things for me
  and holy is his name.

Luke 1:46-49

My soul glorifies the Lord
  and my spirit rejoices in God my Saviour,
for he has been mindful
  of the humble state of his servant.
From now on all generations will call me blessed,
  for the Mighty One has done great things for me—
  holy is his name.

Christmas is panto season—at least, it is in Britain. It's very hard to describe the phenomenon of "pantomime" to non-Brits. I usually suggest that people think of everything they know about British character: reserved, polite, stiff upper lip, emotionally repressed... Then imagine the exact opposite of that and put it on a stage.

One of the common themes of pantomimes is a rags-to-riches tale. Every year, somewhere in a British theatre there will be a retelling of Jack and the Beanstalk, the story of a poor boy discovering great riches. Or Aladdin, the street urchin who becomes a prince. But perhaps the greatest rags-to-riches story of them all is Cinderella: the downtrodden, despised, put-upon girl, living her life in the cinders of the kitchen fire, who transforms into a beautiful princess and marries the prince.

Our first Christmas song, Mary's Magnificat, is a version of the Cinderella story. It's a rags-to-riches tale. Mary starts at the bottom. God "has been mindful of the humble state of his servant," she says (Luke 1:48). This is not a humble brag! God hasn't picked out Mary because of her exemplary humility. She's speaking of her plight rather than her virtue. Mary's not simply humble; she's humbled—even humiliated. She belongs to a defeated nation, under foreign occupation. She lives in a remote backwater in that nation, despised by the cultural elites in the capital. Plus, she's a young woman in a patriarchal society. Her voice doesn't count.

But look again. "All generations will call me blessed," she declares (v 48). She will be honoured for generations to come. We know this isn't empty rhetoric because here we are, retelling her story in *our* generation. Every school Nativity play is another reminder that each new generation still calls Mary "blessed". Galileans like Mary were despised by the Jewish establishment in Jerusalem, and the Jewish establishment was despised by the imperial authorities in Rome. From every angle, Mary is a nobody in the eyes of this world. Yet God has chosen a nobody to be the beginning of something very special.

The first reason that Mary glorifies the Lord (the first "for" in these verses) is that "he has been mindful of the humble state of his servant" (v 48). This could be translated "looked upon" or "noticed". Nobody at the centre of political power in Rome nor the centre of religious power in Jerusalem had heard of Mary. Not many people in her own village would have known her name. Like millions of ordinary people across the world, Mary doesn't matter to others. She's overlooked by the powerful and the wealthy—but not by God. God has been attentive to her humble state.

The only other time that the word "mindful" is used in Luke's Gospel is in Luke 9:38: "Teacher, I beg you to look at [be mindful of] my son, for he is my only child". A man with a demon-possessed boy wants Jesus to notice his son's plight. Jesus does notice and heals the boy. God has noticed the plight of Mary, and he notices the plight of people like her.

The second reason that Mary rejoices (the second "for") is that "the Mighty One has done great things for me". It's the angel Gabriel who has declared those great things to Mary in the story of the *annunciation* (from the Latin word for "announcement"). Lowly Mary is about to give birth to "the Son of the Most High" (1:32). It's a dramatic reversal of fortunes.

God has chosen Mary *despite* her humble origins. But more than that, God has chosen Mary *because* of her humble origins. Her one qualification for being the mother of our Lord is that she has no qualifications! God takes the lowly and works through the weak to magnify his own grace and glory. This is why Mary adds, "[And] holy is his name." This is not a human way of operating; this can only be God at work. In choosing Mary, God is doing something that no one would ever dream of doing.

Mary had no voice. No one had time for her point of view. Yet who's speaking the words which we're reading today? Mary! Her voice echoes down across the centuries and reaches up to heaven.

Mary is humbled, lowly, insignificant. Maybe that's how you feel this Christmas. Remember: God notices. When Hagar—another pregnant woman—was on the run from the torments of her mistress, God met her in the wilderness to reassure her. So Hagar named God, "You are the God who sees me" (Genesis 16:13). God meets you today in his word. God sees you today, even when no one else notices you. And God gives you a voice—a voice he wants to hear.

Reflection

Amidst the vast scene of the world's problems and tragedies you may feel that your own ministry seems so small, so insignificant, so concerned with the trivial. What a tiny difference it can make to the world that you should run a youth club, or preach to a few people in a church, or visit families with seemingly small result. But consider: the glory of Christianity is its claim that small things really matter and that the small company, the very few, the one man, the one woman, the one child are of infinite worth to God ... The Gospel you preach affects the salvation of the world, and you may help your people to influence the world's problems. But you will never be nearer to Christ than in caring for the one man, the one woman, the one child. His authority will be given to you as you do this, and his joy will be yours as well.[2]

Archbishop Michael Ramsey
(1904-1988)

2

Reversed

Magnificat

He has mercy on those who fear him,
from generation to generation.

He has shown strength with his arm
and has scattered the proud in their conceit,

Casting down the mighty from their thrones
and lifting up the lowly.

He has filled the hungry with good things
and sent the rich away empty.

Luke 1:50-53

His mercy extends to those who fear him,
   from generation to generation.
He has performed mighty deeds with his arm;
   he has scattered those who are proud in their
      inmost thoughts.

He has brought down rulers from their thrones
  but has lifted up the humble.
He has filled the hungry with good things
  but has sent the rich away empty.

There's a second Cinderella character in Mary's song: *you*. If you're a Christian, Mary sings of *your* rags-to-riches story. Mary speaks of God's people as "humble" in Luke 1:52. It's the same language that she used to describe herself in verse 48. And Mary calls Israel God's "servant" in verse 54. Again, it's the same word she used to describe herself. The song moves from her experience to our experience. What God has done for Mary is what God is going to do for all his people—including you.

As well as being inspired by the Holy Spirit, Mary's song is also shaped by holy Scripture. The Magnificat is informed by the stories of the mothers of Israel like Sarah, Rebekah, Rachel and Elizabeth—all of them barren women who were gifted a child after a long period of infertility. At key moments in the story, God has fulfilled his purposes through barren women. It's his gentle way of reminding us that his plans don't rely on human power. With the incarnation of Immanuel, he goes one better: now he fulfils his purposes through a virgin.

Sarah, Abraham's wife, laughs at the news that she'll have a child in her old age (Genesis 18:12). She thinks it's a joke. The Lord responds, "Is anything too hard for the LORD?" (v 14). Now Gabriel answers that question: "Nothing will be impossible with God" (Luke 1:37, ESV). God can deliver his promises—even the biggest promise of all: the coming of God himself to earth in the person of Christ.

But perhaps above all, the Magnificat is informed by Hannah's story. Hannah was one of two wives. She was married to Elkanah, whom she shared with another wife called Peninnah. And Peninnah had all the children, while Hannah had none. Not only that but "her rival kept provoking her in order to irritate her" (1 Samuel 1:6). So Hannah prayed for a son, pledging to dedicate him to the Lord's service. Sure enough, the Lord granted Hannah a son whom she sent to serve in the tabernacle. His name was Samuel. Both Hannah and Mary are given a miraculous pregnancy. Hannah's child anointed David, Israel's greatest king. Mary's child is Jesus, the man who would become Israel's ultimate and eternal King. And both Hannah and Mary respond in songs that have a number of striking similarities (2:1-10).

Both Hannah and Mary see their personal stories as a pattern for all of God's people. Both songs contain a series of reversals in which God "brings low and he exalts" (2:7, ESV). God has taken two neglected women and transformed their fortunes. In Mary's case, he'll do this by sending Jesus.

And this transformation is what God is going to do for his people as a whole. Mary speaks of these reversals as past events. There may be a sense in which she looks back to Israel's history to strengthen her hope in God's future. But this is also a prophetic past tense—Mary is speaking of future events as if they've already happened.

A day is coming when this world will be turned upside down. Wealth, celebrity and power will all count for nothing. Corrupt rulers will be toppled, and the arrogant thoughts of those who defend them will be exposed. God is pictured as a mighty warrior marching into battle against oppression (Luke 1:51). The Victorian preacher Charles Spurgeon says,

"Divine providence is like a wheel, and as the wheel revolves, that spoke which was highest becomes the lowest, and that which was lowest is elevated to the highest place".[3]

Not every wealthy or powerful person will be excluded from God's kingdom, just as not every poor person will be included. The reversals of verses 51-53 are introduced by this phrase: "His mercy extends to *those who fear him*" (v 50)—that is, those who humble themselves before God, whether rich or poor. Nevertheless, one day the fundamental structures of this world will be transformed.

Reflection

Mary was a poor Cinderella whom nobody wanted to regard, but God regarded her. And now she will be called blessed by friend and foe, by angels and devils … This song will be sung unceasingly. From the cradle children will be taught this confession of faith: "conceived by the Holy Spirit, born of the Virgin Mary" —that she who is called the Virgin Mary is also a mother. So no one should be afraid, even if you had tough times growing up or you are miserable and despised. It is not a bad omen. Look at Mary's example. And look at what God made out of her![4]

Martin Luther
(1483-1546)

3

Lifted

Magnificat

*Casting down the mighty from their thrones
and lifting up the lowly.*

*He has filled the hungry with good things
and sent the rich away empty.*

Luke 1:52-53

*He has brought down rulers from their thrones
but has lifted up the humble.
He has filled the hungry with good things
but has sent the rich away empty.*

A day is coming when God will bring down the proud and lift up the humble. And Mary's story is a template for this coming reversal. Breaking the oppression of the powerful and righting the wrongs of history on a global scale might seem like the biggest possible transformation there could be. But this song is about something even bigger and even deeper: ending the curse of sin.

Mary speaks of herself and her people as those who've been humbled under God's judgment. The people of Israel were living under the judgment of exile, the ultimate curse that fell on those who were unfaithful (Deuteronomy 28:64-68). Even though they had returned to their land, they still lived under foreign rule, and so they still saw themselves as slaves (Nehemiah 9:36). But we all live under the deeper curse of exile from Eden. Adam and Eve were banished from the presence of God, and ever since, human beings have been struggling to find our way home.

But this movement away from God begins to shift with Mary's child. Jesus is the one who will lead us home to God. Mary's story (along with Hannah's story) is not simply the *template* for our stories; her story is the *turning point* in our stories. It is Jesus who will reverse our fortunes.

Mary may be under judgment of exile but she begins by rejoicing in God as her "Saviour" (Luke 1:47). Salvation is the opposite—the undoing of judgment. And Mary may be under the curse of exile, but she declares, "All generations will call me blessed" (v 48). Blessing is the opposite—the undoing of the curse. God has not only noticed us in our lowly, judged, cursed state; he has stepped in to lift us up. He's written himself into the story of history to take it in a whole new direction. God is sending a Saviour to pay the price of sin and remove the curse of exile.

The opening words of the angel to Mary are "Greetings, you who are highly favoured! The Lord is with you" (v 28). "Do not be afraid, Mary, you have found favour with God" (v 30). The words translated "favoured" and "favour" are variations on the word "grace"; *You have been graced by God*, says the angel. The angel goes on: "You will conceive and give birth to a son, and you are to call him Jesus". The name "Jesus" means "the Lord saves". Mary has been chosen to be the mother of the one who will be the Saviour of the world.

Grace has been given to Mary. And through Mary, grace comes to us because her child becomes our Saviour. Writing to Titus, the apostle Paul says, "The grace of God has appeared" (Titus 2:11). The grace of God appeared in the person of Jesus. He is Love incarnate. Grace comes to us through Mary because she was the one who carried the Son of God in human flesh.

Humanity was exiled from God because Eve had said yes to the serpent. But now Mary has said yes to God. "Adam named his wife Eve because she would become the mother of all the living" (Genesis 3:20). But Eve also played her part in the coming of death into the world. Now Mary is going to be the one through whom Life enters the world. The Spirit overshadows Mary just as the Spirit hovered over creation, poised to breathe life into all that God had made (Genesis 1:2; 2:7). The Puritan Stephen Charnock says that at creation, the Holy Spirit "was brooding upon the chaos, shadowing it with his wings, as hens sit upon their eggs to form them and hatch them", And that at the incarnation, "the Holy Spirit ... overshadowed the Virgin and by a creative act framed the humanity of Christ and united it to the divinity."[5] Elizabeth's words to Mary, "Blessed is the child you will bear", are literally "Blessed is the fruit of your womb" (Luke 1:42). Mary is about to bear fruit, just as humanity was supposed to do (Genesis 1:28). She is about to give birth to one who is the resurrection and the life (John 11:25). Already, in Nazareth, the curse is beginning to wind back towards blessings.

We speak of Adam and Eve's first sin as the "fall" of humanity. Humanity was made to live with God, but we fell from this exalted status. We tumbled down and started plunging toward the depths of hell. But through Mary's son, God "has lifted up the humble" (Luke 1:52). Jesus lifts us up above the stars.

Reflection

Hail the Heav'nly Prince of Peace!
Hail the Sun of Righteousness!
Light and Life to All he brings,
Ris'n with Healing in his Wings.
Mild he lays his Glory by,
Born – that Man no more may die,
Born – to raise the Sons of Earth,
Born – to give them Second Birth.

From "Hark, the Herald Angels Sing"
Charles Wesley
(1707–1788)

4

Beginnings

Magnificat

*Casting down the mighty from their thrones
and lifting up the lowly.*

*He has filled the hungry with good things
and sent the rich away empty.*

Luke 1:52-53

*He has brought down rulers from their thrones
   but has lifted up the humble.
He has filled the hungry with good things
   but has sent the rich away empty.*

Let's take a step back and see where Mary's song has led us. The pride of humanity is in pieces, and corrupt rulers have been dethroned. God's humbled people are lifted up, and the hungry are satisfied. That all sounds rather wonderful. But what's it got to do with real life? Maybe people go from rags to riches in fairy stories, but what does Mary's song speak into our lives with all their disappointments and our world with all its pain?

I wonder if you've ever had this experience: you've been watching a detective drama when the culprit is revealed and an arrest is made. But then you look at the time and notice there's still an hour to go—so you know immediately that they've got the wrong person. There must be another twist. They're yet to find the true culprit. *The story isn't over yet.* (I'll let you in on a secret: in real life the police can't check whether they've arrested the right person by seeing how long there is to go.)

In the same way, when we look at our world, it's easy to think that the way things are now is the way it's going to end. Proud rulers remain on the throne. The greedy continue to have it easy. God's people stay humbled. At this point in the story, Mary's song can grate a bit. Singing "he has filled the hungry with good things" and "lifted up the humble" rings hollow when Christians are among those caught up in famine or when they languish in prison for their faith.

But Mary's song is God's way of pointing to the time, reminding us that *the story isn't over yet*. We've not yet got to the final chapter. There's one dramatic twist to come—a twist to eclipse anything in a Christmas soap-opera special! Jesus is going to turn the whole world upside down. "This child is destined to cause the falling and rising of many in Israel," says Simeon in Luke 2:34. The way things look now is not the way things will be when the credits roll.

The exposure of the proud who reject God and the toppling of rulers who abuse their power lie in the future. On that day, "all those who exalt themselves will be humbled, and those who humble themselves will be exalted" (14:11; see also 13:30).

It begins with Mary. Humbled Mary has been exalted.

It begins with the ministry of Jesus. Jesus welcomes children and touches the outcasts. He feeds the hungry and honours the lowly. He demonstrates divine grace as he eats with sinners. His life is a portrait of a glorious future.

It begins in the church. Your church may not look very impressive—but that's the point! God has chosen the weak and lowly to shame the wise and powerful (1 Corinthians 1:26-29). The church is a home for lost and broken people. The reversal which Mary celebrates and the future which she promises take concrete form in the life of the church.

And it can begin in your home. Just as the meals of Jesus were a sign of his upside-down kingdom, so our meals should display the same upside-down grace. Your Christmas can be a little sign of Christ's coming kingdom as you welcome the lonely and provide for the needy. The New Testament scholar Richard Hays comments, "Luke portrays Jesus and his followers as carrying out the inversion prophesied in Mary's song at the beginning of the Gospel ... This is not to say that they were revolutionaries in the ordinary sense; rather, they are emissaries of a new order of things."[6]

But the place where this needs to begin first of all is in your heart. To share in the future which Mary promises, to be lifted up into the presence of the Most High God, we first need to humble ourselves. We need to admit our need and come to God for his favour and grace.

I can't guarantee that every hungry Christian will be filled this Christmas. I can't guarantee that every persecuted believer will be vindicated. Not this Christmas. Not yet. Maybe not in this life. But we will be filled in the life to come. We will be honoured at the end of the story. When the credits roll, our names will be there.

Reflection

Once in royal David's city
Stood a lowly cattle shed,
Where a mother laid her baby
In a manger for his bed:
Mary was that Mother mild,
Jesus Christ her little Child.

And our eyes at last shall see him
Through his own redeeming love,
For that Child so dear and gentle,
Is our Lord in heaven above:
And he leads his children on
To the place where he is gone.

From "Once in Royal David's City"
Cecil F. Alexander
(1823-1895)

5

Servant

Magnificat

*He has come to the aid of his servant Israel,
to remember his promise of mercy,*

Luke 1:54

*He has helped his servant Israel,
remembering to be merciful.*

For many of us, Christmas is a fun time with family. But for a lot of people, it's tinged with sadness. It brings back memories of loved ones we've lost; some feel their loneliness all the more. It reminds us that life is fragile and the future is uncertain.

Mary has left us looking forward to a day of reversals. Everything that's wrong about this world is one day going to be turned upside down. What happened to Mary herself is the pattern. But frankly, if I'm going to stake my life on a fairy-tale ending like this, I need a bit more to go on. Will I be like Mary, lifted up to be blessed for ever? It feels too good to be true. How can I be sure? How can I face a fragile future with confidence?

Mary has an answer for us, or at least the hint of an answer. She reminds us that Israel was called to be the servant of the Lord: "He has helped his servant Israel, remembering to be merciful" (v 54). The nation of Israel was called to be the servant of God, but Israel failed in that calling. Instead of making the ways of the Lord known to the nations, she followed the ways of the nations. Instead of being a light, she was enveloped in their darkness. Instead of glorifying God, she defamed his name.

So Isaiah promised a coming Servant of the Lord: one who would both fulfil Israel's calling and reverse Israel's failure (Isaiah 42:1-7). So when Mary sings, "He has helped his servant", she's talking about Israel, but she's also talking about Jesus himself. Jesus is the promised Servant: the one who would restore Israel and be the servant that Israel was meant to be (Matthew 12:15-21). Jesus embodies the fortunes of his people. He is our representative—the people of God all wrapped up in one person.

Jesus, the King's Son, left the glory of the palace, stooping low to meet us where we are, so that he can lift us up with him to the throne. We must be humble to accept Christ's help; but first he must be humble to meet us in our need. And that's what he has done.

The English like to remind anyone who will listen that we won the soccer World Cup in 1966. Except of course "we" didn't win it. It was actually eleven footballers who won that day. But the English feel invested in their achievement. Those players won on our behalf, and we share their victory. Jesus fights a battle to the death and wins a great victory over sin. Meanwhile, we're in the stadium, as it were, looking on. But we're invested in his victory. He fights for us as our representative. And so, when Jesus rises from the tomb, we all cheer and hug one another. "We've won, we've won," we can cry. Jesus is the champion who wins the victory for us.

At the cross and resurrection, Jesus underwent the ultimate reversal. First, he went from riches to rags. Having left the glory of heaven, he was exiled from God at the cross—cursed, cast down, humbled. But, three days later, he rose from the tomb—blessed, exalted, honoured. And if we're part of his people by faith, we rise with him. We can face the future with confidence because we have seen the future—our future—in the resurrection of Jesus.

Reflection

*Christ Jesus ... being in very nature God,
did not consider equality with God
something to be used to his own advantage;
rather, he made himself nothing
by taking the very nature of a servant,
being made in human likeness.
And being found in appearance as a man,
he humbled himself
by becoming obedient to death—
even death on a cross!*

*Therefore God exalted him to the highest place
and gave him the name that is above every name,*

*that at the name of Jesus every knee should bow,
in heaven and on earth and under the earth,
and every tongue acknowledge that Jesus Christ is Lord,
to the glory of God the Father.*

Philippians 2:5-11

6

Temple

Luke 1:34-35

"How will this be," Mary asked the angel, "since I am a virgin?" The angel answered, "The Holy Spirit will come on you, and the power of the Most High will overshadow you. So the holy one to be born will be called the Son of God.

As you read these words, there's every chance that you're waiting for a parcel to arrive through the post. Perhaps you've ordered a new handbag for granny and a football for your son. (Don't get those presents mixed up.) And now you're waiting for them to arrive.

Why are you waiting? Why haven't you given up and explored other options? Probably because the online shop from where you bought your presents sent you an email confirming they were on the way. They've promised to deliver your goods, and so you wait with expectation.

Mary's song has left us waiting for the day when the humble will be lifted up. But why go on waiting? Why not give up and explore other options? Because God has promised to deliver.

Look back with me at Mary's story. When Gabriel tells Mary she's bearing God's Son, she asks, "How will this be … since I am a virgin?" (v 34). Gabriel replies, "The Holy Spirit will come on you, and the power of the Most High will overshadow you" (v 35). That's an odd way of putting it. But Gabriel is smart. He's reminding us of something. The word translated "overshadow" is the same word that is used in Exodus 40:35 in the Greek translation of the Old Testament (which the NIV translates as "settled"): "Then the cloud covered the tent of meeting, and the glory of the LORD filled the tabernacle. Moses could not enter the tent of meeting because the cloud had *settled* on [overshadowed] it, and the glory of the LORD filled the tabernacle" (v 34-35; see also Numbers 9:22). These words come at the climax of a long account of the building of the tabernacle and its consecration. Once everything was in place, God himself came down to dwell among his people.

Now Gabriel says, "The power of the Most High will overshadow you". And the last time that happened, the glory of the Lord overshadowed and descended to fill the tabernacle. So what about now with Mary? The power of God is overshadowing Mary, and the glory of God is descending into her womb in the embryonic humanity of the Son of God. Mary's own body is about to become a temple for the living God, for the Word-made-flesh! Cells are splitting to form an embryo as the invisible God takes on a human nature and forms in Mary's womb.

So, the Word of God—in the sense of the divine person—dwells in Mary's womb. But the word of God—

in the sense of the divine promise—also dwells in Mary's heart. "I am the Lord's servant," she tells Gabriel. "May your word to me be fulfilled" (Luke 1:38). Mary gladly submits to God's word, even though it is about to turn her world upside down. Elizabeth blesses her because she "has believed that the Lord would fulfil his promises to her!" (v 45). When the shepherds relay the message of the angels after the birth of Jesus, Luke tells us, "Mary treasured up all these things and pondered them in her heart" (2:19).

Mary is a *symbolic* model for us as she willingly bears God's Word (the divine person) in her womb. And she's a *literal* model for us as she ponders God's word (the divine promise) in her heart. God comes to dwell with us as his word dwells in our hearts.

And through that word, Christ gives us his presence by his Spirit and promises to sustain us as we wait for his coming.

Later in Luke's Gospel, a woman comes to Jesus and declares, "Blessed is the mother who gave you birth and nursed you" (11:27). That's true enough. Elizabeth declares, "Blessed are you among women" (1:42). Mary herself says that "all generations will call me blessed" (v 48). But the response of Jesus in Luke 11 points beyond Mary to those who follow her example. He replies, "Blessed rather are those who hear the word of God and obey it" (v 28). Mary begins her song by declaring that she is blessed (1:48), and you can share in her blessing if you hear God's word and obey it.

Reflection

O holy Child of Bethlehem,
Descend to us, we pray;
Cast out our sin and enter in;
Be born in us today.
We hear the Christmas angels,
The great glad tidings tell;
O come to us, abide with us,
Our Lord Emmanuel!

From "O Little Town of Bethlehem"
Phillips Brooks
(1835–1893)

7

Mercy

Magnificat

He has mercy on those who fear him,
from generation to generation …

He has come to the aid of his servant Israel,
to remember his promise of mercy,

The promise made to our ancestors,
to Abraham and his children for ever.

Luke 1:50, 54-55

His mercy extends to those who fear him,
    from generation to generation …
He has helped his servant Israel,
    remembering to be merciful
to Abraham and his descendants for ever,
    just as he promised our ancestors.

Father Christmas is supposed to bring presents to all the good little boys and girls, though how this operation is managed is never spelt out. What's the standard by which children are judged? How many tidy bedrooms does it take to win a present from Santa? Do toddler tantrums and teenage tiffs cancel out any credit that's been accrued? And for that matter, how does Santa know? We often joke about the logistical operation involved in delivering presents to every home. But have you considered the surveillance operation required to keep tabs on every child? Perhaps Santa has hacked our devices to monitor our conversations. Or perhaps the "elf on the shelf" is actually a whole army of elves on shelves.

People sometimes think of God like this—as a great spy-in-the-sky, constantly monitoring us so he can award presents to all the good little boys and girls.

Mary's song has a different refrain. We've seen how Mary moves from her experience in verses 46-49 to the experience of God's people in verses 51-53. Each of these halves concludes with a kind of chorus with a shared theme: God's mercy. The word "mercy" is repeated in verses 50 and 54 ("remembering to be merciful" in the NIV is literally "to remember mercy"). God is coming in salvation not because we deserve anything from him but because it's in his nature to show mercy. The carol "O Holy Night" suggests that when Christ appeared, "the soul felt its worth".[7] The implication seems to be that a soul is worth the coming of God into the world. Mary, however, sings not of our worth but of God's mercy.

"But when the kindness and love of God our Saviour appeared," says Paul in Titus 3:4-5, "he saved us, not because of righteous things we had done, but because of his mercy". The event Paul is describing—the appearance of God's kindness—is taking place as Mary sings her song. The kindness of God appeared in the humanity of Jesus. God's love is taking on flesh as Mary sings. God himself is coming to rescue his people. Why? Not because of anything we have done but simply "because of his mercy".

You may think you need to win God's approval, but instead God reaches out to you in love. His love for you is on display at Christmas. It takes shape in Mary's womb. It's billboarded in the manger.

The Magnificat introduces us to a God who is characterised both by might and by mercy. God is *able* to save you when you call on him because he's mighty, and God is *willing* to save you because he's merciful.

Zechariah will elaborate on the theme of God's faithfulness to his promises in his song, the Benedictus. For now, notice how the Magnificat moves through time:

- "From now on all generations will call me blessed" (Luke 1:48).

- "His mercy extends to those who fear him, from generation to generation" (v 50).

- "… remembering to be merciful to Abraham and his descendants for ever" (v 54-55).

God's mercy moves down through the generations from Abraham to Isaac to Jacob and on and on until it reaches Mary. And God's mercy continues to move down the generations "from now on" and "for ever". Today, it has reached *your* door. The message of Jesus is proclaimed in our generation. Today, God is still faithful to his promises. Today, God offers you mercy to meet your needs and cover your sins.

For today's reflection I've adapted the Magnificat so that you make it your own as an individual Christian. The bolded text indicates either changes I've made or extra lines I've added.

Reflection

My soul proclaims the greatness of the Lord,
my spirit rejoices in God my Saviour;
he has looked with favour on his lowly servant.
From this day all generations will call me blessed;
the Almighty has done great things for me
and holy is his name.

Lord, thank you for looking with favour on Mary.
I bless her for bearing the Word-made-flesh in her womb.
My spirit rejoices that through her child,
I have been blessed for all generations.
You have done great things for me in Christ,
and holy is your name.

You have *mercy on those who fear* ***you,***
from generation to generation.
You have *shown strength with* ***your*** *arm*
and ***have*** *scattered the proud in their conceit,*
casting down the mighty from their thrones
and lifting up the lowly.
You have *filled the hungry with good things*
and sent the rich away empty.

*Lord, I rejoice that a day is coming
when you will right every wrong.
I humble myself before you
and put my faith in your mercy.*

*You **have** come to the aid of your servant **people**,
through the aid of your Servant Jesus,
to remember **your** promise of mercy,
the promise made to **my** ancestors **in the faith**,
to Abraham and his children for ever.
And holy is your name.*

Zechariah's Song:
The Benedictus

Blessed be the Lord the God of Israel,
who has come to his people and set them free.

He has raised up for us a mighty Saviour,
born of the house of his servant David.

Through his holy prophets God promised of old
to save us from our enemies,
*   from the hands of all that hate us,*

To show mercy to our ancestors,
and to remember his holy covenant.

This was the oath God swore to our father Abraham:
to set us free from the hands of our enemies,

Free to worship him without fear,
holy and righteous in his sight
*   all the days of our life.*

And you, child, shall be called
*   the prophet of the Most High,*
for you will go before the Lord to prepare his way,

To give his people knowledge of salvation
by the forgiveness of all their sins.

*In the tender compassion of our God
the dawn from on high shall break upon us,*

*To shine on those who dwell in darkness
   and the shadow of death,
and to guide our feet into the way of peace.*

Luke 1:5-25, 57-79

[5] In the time of Herod king of Judea there was a priest named Zechariah, who belonged to the priestly division of Abijah; his wife Elizabeth was also a descendant of Aaron. [6] Both of them were righteous in the sight of God, observing all the Lord's commands and decrees blamelessly. [7] But they were childless because Elizabeth was not able to conceive, and they were both very old.

[8] Once when Zechariah's division was on duty and he was serving as priest before God, [9] he was chosen by lot, according to the custom of the priesthood, to go into the temple of the Lord and burn incense. [10] And when the time for the burning of incense came, all the assembled worshippers were praying outside.

[11] Then an angel of the Lord appeared to him, standing at the right side of the altar of incense. [12] When Zechariah saw him, he was startled and was gripped with fear. [13] But the angel said to him: "Do not be afraid, Zechariah; your prayer has been heard. Your wife Elizabeth will bear you a son, and you are to call him John. [14] He will be a joy and delight to you, and many will rejoice because of his birth, [15] for he will be great in the sight of the Lord. He is never to take wine or other

fermented drink, and he will be filled with the Holy Spirit even before he is born. [16] *He will bring back many of the people of Israel to the Lord their God.* [17] *And he will go on before the Lord, in the spirit and power of Elijah, to turn the hearts of the parents to their children and the disobedient to the wisdom of the righteous—to make ready a people prepared for the Lord."*

[18] *Zechariah asked the angel, "How can I be sure of this? I am an old man and my wife is well on in years."*

[19] *The angel said to him, "I am Gabriel. I stand in the presence of God, and I have been sent to speak to you and to tell you this good news.* [20] *And now you will be silent and not able to speak until the day this happens, because you did not believe my words, which will come true at their appointed time."*

[21] *Meanwhile, the people were waiting for Zechariah and wondering why he stayed so long in the temple.* [22] *When he came out, he could not speak to them. They realised he had seen a vision in the temple, for he kept making signs to them but remained unable to speak.*

[23] *When his time of service was completed, he returned home.* [24] *After this his wife Elizabeth became pregnant and for five months remained in seclusion.* [25] *"The Lord has done this for me," she said. "In these days he has shown his favour and taken away my disgrace among the people"* …

[57] *When it was time for Elizabeth to have her baby, she gave birth to a son.* [58] *Her neighbours and relatives heard that the Lord had shown her great mercy, and they shared her joy.*

⁵⁹ On the eighth day they came to circumcise the child, and they were going to name him after his father Zechariah, ⁶⁰ but his mother spoke up and said, "No! He is to be called John."

⁶¹ They said to her, "There is no one among your relatives who has that name."

⁶² Then they made signs to his father, to find out what he would like to name the child. ⁶³ He asked for a writing tablet, and to everyone's astonishment he wrote, "His name is John." ⁶⁴ Immediately his mouth was opened and his tongue set free, and he began to speak, praising God. ⁶⁵ All the neighbours were filled with awe, and throughout the hill country of Judea people were talking about all these things. ⁶⁶ Everyone who heard this wondered about it, asking, "What then is this child going to be?" For the Lord's hand was with him.

⁶⁷ His father Zechariah was filled with the Holy Spirit and prophesied:

⁶⁸ "Praise be to the Lord, the God of Israel,
    because he has come to his people and
      redeemed them.
⁶⁹ He has raised up a horn of salvation for us
    in the house of his servant David
⁷⁰ (as he said through his holy prophets of long ago),
⁷¹ salvation from our enemies
    and from the hand of all who hate us—
⁷² to show mercy to our ancestors
    and to remember his holy covenant,
    ⁷³ the oath he swore to our father Abraham:

⁷⁴ *to rescue us from the hand of our enemies,*
   and to enable us to serve him without fear
⁷⁵ *in holiness and righteousness before him*
   all our days.

⁷⁶ *And you, my child, will be called a prophet*
   of the Most High;
   for you will go on before the Lord to prepare
   the way for him,
⁷⁷ *to give his people the knowledge of salvation*
   through the forgiveness of their sins,
⁷⁸ *because of the tender mercy of our God,*
   by which the rising sun will come to us
   from heaven
⁷⁹ *to shine on those living in darkness*
   and in the shadow of death,
to guide our feet into the path of peace."

Prophecy

Luke 1:13-22

The angel said to him: "Do not be afraid, Zechariah; your prayer has been heard. Your wife Elizabeth will bear you a son, and you are to call him John. He will be a joy and delight to you, and many will rejoice because of his birth, for he will be great in the sight of the Lord. He is never to take wine or other fermented drink, and he will be filled with the Holy Spirit even before he is born. He will bring back many of the people of Israel to the Lord their God. And he will go on before the Lord, in the spirit and power of Elijah, to turn the hearts of the parents to their children and the disobedient to the wisdom of the righteous—to make ready a people prepared for the Lord."

Zechariah asked the angel, "How can I be sure of this? I am an old man and my wife is well on in years."

The angel said to him, "I am Gabriel. I stand in the presence of God, and I have been sent to speak to you

*and to tell you this good news. And now you will be
silent and not able to speak until the day this happens,
because you did not believe my words, which will come
true at their appointed time."*

*Meanwhile, the people were waiting for Zechariah and
wondering why he stayed so long in the temple.
When he came out, he could not speak to them. They
realised he had seen a vision in the temple, for he kept
making signs to them but remained unable to speak.*

Zechariah has reached the high point of his career. His normal day-job as a country priest was to teach the people in his local community, but today he's been chosen to offer incense in the temple in Jerusalem. With several thousand priests in Judea, for him this is a once-in-a-lifetime occasion.

And then Zechariah meets an angel! For 400 years God has been silent. No prophecies. No visions. Nothing. But today Zechariah is standing face to face with an angel. It's not immediately clear whether this is good news—Zechariah's "gripped with fear" (v 12). But the angel says Zechariah and his wife will have the longed-for baby they thought would never come. "He will be a joy and delight to you," says Gabriel (v 14). But then it gets weird and then weirder still.

Gabriel says, "Many will rejoice because of his birth, for he will be great in the sight of the Lord" (v 14-15) and adds that the boy is not to drink any alcohol. Back in the Old Testament, Israelites could make a special "Nazirite" vow, which included temporary abstinence—both from alcohol and haircuts (Numbers 6:1-6). It was a sign of dedication to God. Zechariah's thoughts would have gone to Samson, the mighty hero who had rescued God's people from the Philistines. An angel had come to Samson's parents, who, like Zechariah and Elizabeth, were childless, and were promised a son who would be a permanent Nazirite (Judges 13:2-7). So perhaps Zechariah's boy was going to be a new Samson, wholly dedicated to God.

Zechariah's thoughts would also have gone to Hannah, the childless woman who was promised a child in the tabernacle—the precursor to the temple in which Zechariah now stood. Hannah had made a Nazirite vow on behalf of her as yet unconceived son (1 Samuel 1:11). Hannah's child was the prophet Samuel, and it was Samuel who later anointed David, Israel's greatest king. So perhaps Zechariah's boy was going to be a new Samuel, anointing a new king.

Gabriel continues, "He will be filled with the Holy Spirit even before he is born" and "bring back many of the people of Israel to the Lord their God" (Luke 1:15-16). Maybe Zechariah's thoughts were going to the prophet Elijah. Only Gabriel was one step ahead of him: "He will go on before the Lord, in the spirit and power of Elijah" (v 17). Elijah had led Israel back to God, most famously at Mount Carmel, when he staged a contest with the prophets of Baal (1 Kings 18). Now Gabriel was saying that Zechariah's boy would be a new Elijah.

Zechariah would have also heard an echo of the prophet Malachi: "See, I will send the prophet Elijah to you before that great and dreadful day of the LORD comes" (Malachi 4:5). Elijah had been taken up to heaven by a fiery chariot without ever dying. So the Jews thought Elijah might return one day to prepare for the coming of God. If Zechariah's boy was the new Elijah, that would mean something even more astonishing: *God himself was on his way.*

Gabriel tells Zechariah, "Your prayer has been heard" (Luke 1:13). But which prayer is it? His prayer for a child or his prayer that God would save Israel? Or both? Perhaps God was answering Zechariah's prayer for his people by answering his prayer for a child.

The implications are dizzying, and Zechariah loses his spiritual balance. "How can I be sure of this?" he says (v 18). Poor Gabriel. He seems personally affronted. "I am Gabriel," he says. "I stand in the presence of God, and I have been sent to speak to you and to tell you this good news" (v 19). *Don't you know who I am?* Gabriel seems to be saying. *Don't you realise who sent me?*

At this climatic point in his life, Zechariah is brought low. He doesn't believe Gabriel's words, and so words are taken from him (v 20-22). Gabriel visits Zechariah before he visits Mary, but Mary's song comes first because Zechariah's doubt makes him temporarily mute. Zechariah embodies the message of her song: the proud are brought low (v 51-52).

For the first hearers of Zechariah's song, he was announcing in advance what would happen. By the time Luke writes his Gospel, those events have largely happened. So Luke includes this song not to tell us what *will* happen but to explain what *has* happened.

It isn't the end of the line for Zechariah. He learns humility and regains his voice (v 57-66). It's a warning and promise for those born into privilege; we will be brought low unless we voluntarily lower ourselves before God.

Reflection

O little town of Bethlehem,
How still we see thee lie.
Above thy deep and dreamless sleep
The silent stars go by.
Yet in thy dark streets shineth
The everlasting light.
The hopes and fears of all the years
Are met in thee tonight.

From "O Little Town of Bethlehem"
Phillips Brooks
(1835-1893)

9

Coming

Benedictus

Blessed be the Lord the God of Israel,
who has come to his people and set them free.

He has raised up for us a mighty Saviour,
born of the house of his servant David.

Luke 1:68-69

Praise be to the Lord, the God of Israel,
  because he has come to his people
    and redeemed them.
He has raised up a horn of salvation for us
  in the house of his servant David.

Imagine you could recreate events from your life, except that second time round you could do things much better. That work presentation that fell flat? This time round everyone is amazed, and your proposal is applauded. That first date that never became a second date? This time round you're charming and witty—and you don't spill your drink into their lap. Or imagine you could replay events from world history. It's the Battle of Hastings, except this time the arrow misses Harold's eye and William the Conqueror is forever known as William the Defeated.

Zechariah's song retells *the* story from Israel's history—the BIG one, the story of the exodus from slavery in Egypt—and imagines how it might be replayed with a bigger and better outcome. Except this is no idle fantasy; it's what is really about to happen. Luke says that this song is a prophecy inspired by the Holy Spirit, and prophecies inspired by the Holy Spirit always come true (v 67). This is what Jesus is about to accomplish.

When a new building development is proposed, it often comes with an artist's impression—a picture to give a feel for what the finished project will look like. The exodus was God's artist's impression of salvation. God was saying, *When I save humanity, it will look a bit like this—but on a much grander scale.* Zechariah says the real exodus is coming.

Let's start with the first exodus. The Israelites are living in slavery in Egypt. The whole nation has become subjected to a "bitter" life of "harsh labour" (Exodus 1:14). Then the Lord speaks to Moses from a burning bush: "I have indeed seen the misery of my people in Egypt. I have heard them crying out because of their slave drivers, and I am concerned about their suffering. So I have come down to rescue them from the hand of the Egyptians and to bring them up out of that land into a good and spacious land, a land flowing with milk and honey" (3:7-8). That's the first thing you need to know about the exodus: *God comes to his people.*

And how does Zechariah begin? "Blessed be the Lord the God of Israel, who has come to his people". Just as God came to his people in Moses' day, so God is coming to his people in Zechariah's day.

What does that look like? Or rather, *who* does it look like? Zechariah continues, "He has raised up for us a mighty Saviour, born of the house of his servant David". Zechariah is drawing on another strand of Israel's story. God made a covenant with King David in which God promised to adopt David's sons and ensure that they would rule for ever over God's people (2 Samuel 7:11-16). This promise is about to be fulfilled, and the story will be even bigger: God is not simply going to *adopt* David's son—God is going to send *his own Son* as David's successor.

Put it all together and we can see why Zechariah is so excited: God himself has come in the person of his Son, empowered by his Spirit. As Zechariah speaks, Jesus is already present in the womb of Mary.

The first event Luke describes in his Gospel is the angel appearing to Zechariah in the temple, and the last event he describes is the disciples "continually at the temple, praising God" (Luke 1:8-11 and 24:53). So Luke's Gospel begins and ends in the temple. The temple was the place of meeting between God and humanity. Luke frames his Gospel in this way so that we see it as a "place" where we can meet God in Christ.

Each year hundreds of tourists visit St Paul's Cathedral in London to marvel at its classical architecture. Valid as this is (and it is a beautiful building), it misses the point.

The cathedral was built as a place in which to meet God and hear his voice. The same is true of the Bible. We can read the Bible like a tourist traipsing round a cathedral, marvelling at its artistry. That's okay because the Bible is an astonishing cultural artefact. But reading the Bible like this misses the main point; first and foremost, the Bible is a place in which to meet God and to hear his voice. All the patterns and connections in the Bible—all the things that make it amazing literature—are there to lead us to Jesus.

Over the next few days, we'll retrace the story of the exodus—the first exodus illuminating the Jesus exodus. Here are the steps we're going to take:

The First Exodus	The Jesus Exodus
God came down at the burning bush.	God has come down in the person of Christ.
God came down as promised.	God has come in Christ as promised.
God came down to set Israel free.	God has come in Christ to set us free.
God came down to forgive his people.	God has come in Christ to forgive us.
God led Israel to the promised land.	God in Christ is leading us home to God.

Jesus has come to us through his incarnation, and he continues to come to us now in his word through his Holy Spirit. Back at the burning bush, God had said to Moses, "I have seen the misery of my people … I have indeed heard them crying out … I am concerned about their suffering … I have come down to rescue them" (Exodus 3:7-8). Today God says to you, *I have seen your misery. I have heard your cries. I am concerned about your suffering. I have come down to you in Jesus.*

Reflection

Veiled in flesh the Godhead see!
Hail the incarnate Deity!
Pleased as man with men to dwell,
Jesus, our Immanuel.

From "Hark, the Herald Angels Sing"
Adapted from Charles Wesley
(1707-1788)

10

Promised

Benedictus

*Through his holy prophets God promised of old
to save us from our enemies,
    from the hands of all that hate us,*

*To show mercy to our ancestors,
and to remember his holy covenant.*

Luke 1:70-72

*… (as he said through his holy prophets of long ago),
salvation from our enemies
    and from the hand of all who hate us—
to show mercy to our ancestors
    and to remember his holy covenant.*

I'm careful about the promises I make. I don't want to find myself under an obligation I can't keep. So I try to "under-promise" in the hope that I'll be able to "over-deliver". God doesn't do under-promising—his promises are big! But then God never finds himself lumbered with a promise he can't keep.

Zechariah's song is about promises. He's using the exodus story to describe the work of Jesus. First off, God came to his people in the exodus, and now God has come to us in Jesus. The second thing you need to know about the first exodus is that God came *as he promised*. When God heard the Israelites groaning, "he remembered his covenant with Abraham, with Isaac and with Jacob" (Exodus 2:24). When he appeared to Moses, he announced himself as "the God of your fathers—the God of Abraham, the God of Isaac and the God of Jacob" (3:15-17; 4:5; 6:8). God has not only come; he's come as promised.

How does Zechariah continue? "Through his holy prophets God promised of old to save us from our enemies … to remember his holy covenant." What's happening shouldn't be a surprise to those who have diligently read the Scriptures. Luke 1:70 is literally "He spoke by the mouth [singular] of his holy prophets [plural] from of old". All the prophets spoke with one voice. They all pointed to this moment (1 Peter 1:10-12). All the trajectories launched by their words converge in the baby in Mary's womb.

Zechariah has placed a bonus link in Luke 1:71. The two Greek words translated "enemies" and "all that hate us" are the words that the Greek version of the Old Testament uses for "enemy" and "foes" in Psalm 18:17. And Psalm 18 again describes salvation using the imagery from the exodus:

The valleys of the sea were exposed …
at your rebuke, LORD,

> *at the blast of breath from your nostrils.*
> *He reached down from on high and took hold of me;*
> *he drew me out of deep waters.*
> *He rescued me from my powerful enemy,*
> *from my foes, who were too strong for me. (v 15-17)*

What's striking about Psalm 18 is that David is describing his own experience—he doesn't say *rescued us* but *rescued me*. David uses the language of exodus because David sees the exodus as the pattern for God's salvation. Just as God had rescued Israel from Egypt, so God rescued David from his enemies. Zechariah takes this one big step further: through Jesus, God is rescuing his people from the enemies of sin and death.

Zechariah links God keeping his promises with God showing mercy (Luke 1:72). That's because by "mercy", Zechariah has in mind a Hebrew word often translated as "steadfast love" (*hesed*). It describes God's gracious commitment to his covenant. We sometimes talk about the letter of the law and the spirit of the law. Suppose a mother tells her son to say sorry to his sister. So the boy says, "Sooooorry" in a whiny voice. He's kept the letter of the law by uttering the word "sorry". But he's not kept the spirit of his mother's commands. Let's suppose instead he both says, "Sorry" and gives his sister a hug. Now he's kept both the letter and spirit of the law. God keeps the letter of his covenant because he must be true to his words. But he also keeps his covenant because he loves his people. God has covenant obligations, which must be kept, but only because in love he chose to place himself under these obligations. So for God to show steadfast love is to remember his covenant, and to remember his covenant is to show steadfast love (Deuteronomy 7:9; 1 Kings 8:23).

Think what this means when you sin. God is bound by his covenant to forgive you. The Lord's Supper is God's signature on this covenant commitment (Matthew 26:28), and God doesn't do this begrudgingly. He's not like an insurance company paying out simply because a contract requires them to do so. God delights to show mercy to his people. And he delights to show mercy to *you*. That's the reason that he signed up to this covenant in the first place. It's not that we negotiated a good deal; we had no bargaining power. God alone set the terms, and the terms are *mercy*.

When we sin, we can imagine that, while God forgives us because he's obligated to us, he feels fed up with us. We can think he's like the boy saying, "Sooooorry"—keeping the letter of the covenant with a whiny voice that betrays his frustration. Nothing could be further from the truth. God delights to forgive his children. He says, *I forgive you* (that's the letter of the law), *and* he throws his arms around you in love (that's the spirit of his law). He remembers his holy covenant, and he showers us with steadfast love. God has come in Christ, says Zechariah, just as he promised. And God comes to you in mercy, just as he promised.

Reflection

The mercy of God's heart means His hearty mercy, His cordial delight in mercy. Remission of sins is a business into which the Lord throws His heart. He forgives with an intensity of will, and readiness of soul. God made heaven and earth with His fingers, but He gave His Son with His heart in order that He might save sinners. The Eternal God has thrown His whole soul into the business of redeeming men. If you desire to see God most Godlike, it is in the pardon of sin, and the saving of men. If you desire to read the character of God written out in capital letters, you must study the visitation of His love in the person of His dear Son, and all the wonderful works of infinite grace which spring from there.[8]

Charles H. Spurgeon
(1834-1982)

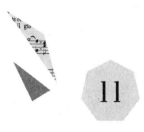

11

Freedom

Benedictus

*This was the oath God swore to our father Abraham:
to set us free from the hands of our enemies,*

*Free to worship him without fear,
holy and righteous in his sight
    all the days of our life.*

Luke 1:73-75

*… the oath he swore to our father Abraham:
to rescue us from the hand of our enemies,
    and to enable us to serve him without fear
    in holiness and righteousness before him all our days.*

God has come as promised. But what is his promise? God saved Israel from slavery in Egypt. But the first exodus wasn't simply "freedom from…" It was also "freedom for…"—freedom to know God, to be his people, and to worship him "all the days of our life". Moses went to Pharaoh with this message from God: "Let my son go, so that he may worship me" (Exodus 4:23). God wasn't simply intervening to liberate an oppressed people. That was true, and it's been an inspiration for freedom movements ever since. But God was also creating a people who would be his people. The goal of the exodus was communion with God. That's why the story told in the book of Exodus doesn't end with liberation for Egypt in chapter 15. It ends 25 chapters later, when the Lord descends in glory on the newly built tabernacle (40:34-38). It only ends once God has come to dwell with his people.

What happens next in the new version of the exodus that Zechariah is celebrating? God has come "to set us free from the hands of our enemies / Free to worship him without fear". These words would have felt very poignant for Luke's first readers because the Jews were still under the tyranny of Roman oppression. But remember, the Jesus exodus is doing something bigger and better than the Moses exodus. God is setting his people free from the great enemies of sin and death.

And through Christ we also enjoy a bigger and better freedom-*for*. We're set free for life as God's children. "Let my son go," God said to Pharaoh at the first exodus. But now "my son" is not just a picture of God's commitment to Israel; "my son" is about to be born into the world. The eternal Son of God is taking on human flesh in the womb of Mary. And Jesus is coming so that you and I can share his father-son relationship with God. He has come that we might be adopted as sons and daughters. This is why we pray, "Our Father"; his Father has become our Father.

But there's a mysterious reversal. When God tells Pharaoh, "Let my son go, so that he may worship me" (4:23), the word translated for "worship" is the same word used to describe "slavery" or "servitude" in Egypt. God's people move from the service of Pharaoh to the service of God. Perhaps that doesn't sound like much of an improvement! But look how Zechariah puts it: God sets us "free to worship him *without fear*". The service of Pharaoh was filled with fear. Every day you would wake up fearing another demand or another beating.

You may not fear a beating, but the things we serve can still fill us with fear. Think about what shapes your behaviour—a longing for acceptance, perhaps. Financial security. Success. Serving these things fills us with fear. Long for acceptance and you will fear rejection. Long for security and you will fear uncertainty. Long for success and you will fear failure. What if we're not good enough? What if you can't make it work?

But we can serve God *without* fear. Why? Because God makes us "holy and righteous in his sight all the days of our life". We're not serving to earn God's approval or secure our future. We already have all those things in Christ. Today, here and now, if you've put your faith in Christ, you're holy and righteous in God's sight. And tomorrow. And the next day. And "all the days of [your] life". There's no need to fear, for perfect love has cast out fear. Let the love of God demonstrated in the cross of Christ cast out your fear this Christmas.

Every time we read the Benedictus, we're being reminded that we've been set free to serve God. But we're also reminded that his service is perfect freedom.

Reflection

Come, thou long-expected Jesus,
Born to set thy people free;
From our fears and sins release us,
Let us find our rest in thee.
Israel's strength and consolation,
Hope of all the earth thou art;
Dear desire of every nation,
Joy of every longing heart.

From "Come, Thou Long-Expected Jesus"
Charles Wesley
(1707–1788)

Forgiveness

Benedictus

*And you, child, shall be called the prophet
   of the Most High,
for you will go before the Lord to prepare his way,*

*To give his people knowledge of salvation
by the forgiveness of all their sins.*

Luke 1:76-77

*And you, my child, will be called a prophet
   of the Most High;
   for you will go on before the Lord to
      prepare the way for him,
to give his people the knowledge of salvation
   through the forgiveness of their sins.*

God has promised that his people will be "holy and righteous in his sight". Perhaps that leaves you with a question—how can God declare me to be "holy and righteous in his sight" when I'm anything but holy and righteous?! What kind of make-believe is this? And how will it stand up in court? Will it protect me on the final day of judgment?

To answer these questions, we need to go back to the exodus story. The exodus was accomplished through a final plague—the death of every firstborn son. The problem was that the Israelites deserved this act of judgment just as much as the Egyptians. But Israelite families escaped this judgment by sacrificing a lamb and daubing its blood over their doors. The lamb symbolically died in their place so that they could be forgiven.

The Israelites were set free, but their hearts weren't changed. They went back to their old ways and ended up in exile all over again. This time Egyptian pharaohs were replaced by Babylonian potentates. So the prophets promised a new exodus.

The first exodus was amazing—an enslaved people overcame the world's greatest superpower. But it didn't go far enough. If we're truly to enjoy freedom-for-God, we need to be forgiven. If we're going to be "holy and righteous in his sight", someone needs to deal with all our guilt. So the prophet Isaiah promised a new exodus—patterned on the first exodus but bigger and better, overcoming sin and conquering death:

Comfort, comfort my people,
  says your God.
Speak tenderly to Jerusalem,
  and proclaim to her

that her hard service has been completed,
 that her sin has been paid for,
that she has received from the LORD's hand
 double for all her sins. (Isaiah 40:1-2)

"Double" here doesn't mean that God will punish our sins twice as much as they deserve! It's the idea of a debt meeting its match. First there's sin; second there's a payment for sin. As a result, their "sin has been paid for". How can we be holy and righteous in God's sight? Because someone is going to pay the price of our sin. Who could it be? I suspect you're one step ahead of me here, but the next words Isaiah speaks are these:

A voice of one calling:
"In the wilderness prepare
 the way for the LORD;
make straight in the desert
 a highway for our God." (v 3)

Zechariah echoes this verse in his song: "And you, child ... will go before the Lord to prepare his way". He's talking about his son, John the Baptist. After all, this song was sung to celebrate John's birth! Ancient cities would prepare for the coming of kings by improving the infrastructure, cleaning the streets and rehearsing the welcome ceremony. John did his own version of this. Except, instead of building roads or sprucing up cities, he prepared people for the coming of God by "preaching a baptism of repentance for the forgiveness of sins" (Luke 3:3).

John was only the warm-up act. He prepared the way for someone else—the one who would pay the price of sin. A day came when he pointed to Jesus and declared,

"Look, the Lamb of God, who takes away the sin of the world!" (John 1:29). Jesus is the true Passover Lamb, who died that we might be forgiven. God's own firstborn Son was born into the world, and 33 years later his blood was shed as a sacrifice for sin. So we can receive the forgiveness that John promises.

Reflection

He was a baby and a child,
so that you may be a perfect human.
He was wrapped in swaddling clothes,
so that you may be freed from the snares of death …
He was on earth
that you may be in the stars.
He had no other place in the inn,
so that you may have many mansions in the heavens.
He, being rich, became poor for your sakes,
that through his poverty you might be rich.
Therefore his poverty is our inheritance,
and the Lord's weakness is our virtue.
He chose to lack for himself,
that he may abound for all.[9]

St Ambrose
(339–397)

13

Dawn

Benedictus

*In the tender compassion of our God
the dawn from on high shall break upon us,*

*To shine on those who dwell in darkness
and the shadow of death,
and to guide our feet into the way of peace.*

Luke 1:78-79

*… because of the tender mercy of our God,
by which the rising sun will come to us from heaven
to shine on those living in darkness
and in the shadow of death,
to guide our feet into the path of peace.*

In a British winter, it gets dark at around four o'clock in the afternoon. Most people go to work in the dark and then come home in the dark. So it's always a delight when spring comes with lighter evenings. But imagine living in continual night-time. Darkness is a picture of life under "the shadow of death". Just as every day ends in darkness, so every life ends in death. We live with death's shadow cast over our lives.

No carol service is complete without a reading from Isaiah 9: "For unto us a child is born, unto us a son is given" (v 6, KJV). It's a reading that begins, "The people walking in darkness have seen a great light; on those living in the land of deep darkness a light has dawned" (v 2). Zechariah seems to have these words in mind as he concludes his song; God is coming in Jesus "to shine on those who dwell in darkness and the shadow of death". Isaiah's prophecy is being fulfilled, says Zechariah. Dawn is about to break across the darkness of a world under sin. Light is about to burst forth, dispelling the deathly shadows that haunt our lives.

The apostle John starts his Gospel with a reference to John the Baptist. "He came as a witness to testify concerning that light," says John 1:7. But then the apostle adds, "He himself was not the light". "The true light that gives light to everyone" is Jesus Christ, the Word become flesh, "the one and only Son, who is himself God" (v 9, 14, 18).

Zechariah makes the same point. "The rising sun," Zechariah says, "will come to us from heaven" (Luke 1:78). This is not a literal dawn. This is Jesus, coming from heaven. The prophet Malachi had promised, "For you who revere my name, the sun of righteousness will rise with healing in its rays" (Malachi 4:2). Jesus the Son is the sun that lights up our future.

Think of the first bright day of summer. Instead of the cold chilling your bones, your limbs relax in the warmth of the sun. Instead of scurrying out of the rain, people chat happily on the street. So it is when we step into the sunshine of Jesus. We relax, we heal, we warm up. Fear and gloom are replaced by life and light.

There may be another Old Testament allusion in these verses. The word "dawn" is literally "rising". It can refer to the rising of the sun, but it can also describe a shoot or branch rising up from a plant. It's the word used in the Greek translation of Jeremiah 23:5: "'The days are coming,' declares the LORD, 'when I will raise up for David a righteous Branch'." Or perhaps Zechariah has in mind the one after whom he would have been named, the prophet Zechariah: "I am going to bring my servant, the Branch." (Zechariah 3:8; 6:12). God had promised that one of David's sons would reign for ever over God's people. Yet it looked as if the line of David had run into the ground with the exile into Babylon. So Isaiah had promised, "A shoot will come up from the stump of Jesse; from his roots a Branch will bear fruit" (Isaiah 11:1). A king would rise from the ruins of exile to restore God's life-giving reign. The sun would appear through the rising up of a new king.

After the first exodus from Egypt, God led his people to a new home in the promised land—a land flowing with milk and honey. It's the same with the Jesus exodus: Jesus is going lead us home to God. Light has dawned "to guide our feet into the way of peace". Imagine walking home in the days before street lamps. You would stumble around, tripping over rocks, bumping into trees, losing your way. But in daylight the way is clear. Jesus reveals God to us like no one else because he himself is God. Jesus has come to light our path and guide us home.

When you board a plane, you will be told (if you bother to listen), "In the event of a crash landing, floor lights will guide you to the exit". Humanity has crash landed into darkness. But Jesus lights the way and guides us to peace. What is this peace? For an answer to that question, we need to wait for the third of Luke's Christmas songs, the Gloria sung by the angels to the shepherds.

Reflection

Zechariah calls Christ the Dayspring from on high, in respect to his divinity, by which he was and is above all creatures. Where there is nothing but only height itself, there is Christ in his divinity, even as the "dayspring" or the sun rising. For he proceeds from the Father even as beams of light proceed from the sun ... As the sun gives light to our bodies, so Christ gives light to our minds. And with this, Zechariah shows why he calls Christ the "Dayspring": namely, because he will lighten those who sit in darkness and in the shadow of death.[10]

Heinrich Bullinger
(1504-1575)

14

Praise

Benedictus

Blessed be the Lord the God of Israel.

Luke 1:68

Praise be to the Lord, the God of Israel.

Here's an experiment you might like to try today: see how long you can go without saying anything. Better still, if you have children, use them as your guinea pigs. Challenge them to see how long they can go without talking. Then perhaps you might have a peaceful day. Or what about a morning? An hour or two? Five minutes? How long do you think you would last?

When Zechariah questions Gabriel's message, he becomes unable to say anything. "He kept making signs to them but remained unable to speak" (v 19-22). Only when John is born is Zechariah able to speak again (v 57-66). But what words they are. Zechariah has spent nine months in silence, turning his thoughts over until they have coalesced into this amazing song.

What have Zechariah's words taught us? They've shown that God has come in Christ as promised, to set us free to worship him through forgiveness and illumination.

We need to consider not only what these verses *say* but also what they *are*. They're poetry. This is a song. All the Old Testament allusions are very interesting. But Zechariah didn't just write these lyrics—inspired by the Holy Spirit and recorded by Luke—as a theological curiosity.

This song tells a story that's meant to make our pulses race and our hearts sing. The opening words are not *The Lord has come*. The opening words are "Praise be to the Lord … because he has come". Zechariah tells us that God is coming in Jesus "to set us free … to worship him … all the days of our life". Zechariah's words are the beginning of the worshipful life God promises.

First and foremost, this song is an exhortation to praise God:

- The God who stooped from the heavens in the person of Christ

- The God who has been faithful to his promises

- The God who has set us free to be his sons and daughters

- The God who submitted himself to a vicious death to pay the price of our sin

- The God who lights up our lives with the warmth of his love

- The God who leads us home

Of course, we can't turn on joyful praise like someone turning on a tap. Whether for good or ill, our words flow from our hearts. "For the mouth speaks what the heart is full of" (Luke 6:43-45). To follow Zechariah's lead, we need to stir our hearts, and that means pausing, reflecting and gazing afresh at the God-man in the manger. Here's the Victorian preacher Charles Spurgeon to get us started:

Pause, Christian, and consider this a minute. See how every attribute is here magnified. Lo! what wisdom is here. God becomes man that God may be just and the justifier of the ungodly. Lo! what power, for where is power so great as when it conceals power? What power, that Godhead should un-robe itself and become man! Behold, what love is thus revealed to us when Jesus becomes a man. Behold ye what faithfulness! How many promises are this day kept? How many solemn obligations are this hour discharged? ... The whole of God is glorified in Christ. And though some part of the name of God is written in the universe, it is best read here—in Him who was the Son of man, and yet, the Son of God.[11]

For today's reflection, I've adapted the Benedictus so you can make it your own as an individual Christian. The core text is the liturgical version with bold text indicating either changes I've made or extra words I've added.

Reflection

Blessed be the Lord the God of Israel,
*who has come to **me** and set **me** free.*
*He has raised up for **me** a mighty Saviour,*
born of the house of his servant David.

Through his holy prophets, God promised of old
*to save **people like me** from our enemies,*
from the hands of all that hate us,
to show mercy to our ancestors,
and to remember his holy covenant.

This was the oath God swore to Abraham,
my** father **in faith:
*to set **me** free from the hands of **my** enemies,*
free to worship him without fear,
*holy and righteous in his sight all the days of **my** life.*

***John the Baptist** was the prophet of the Most High,*
*for **he went** before the Lord **Jesus** to prepare his way,*
*to give **us** knowledge of salvation*
*by the forgiveness of all **our** sins.*

*In the tender compassion of **my** God,*
*the dawn from on high has broken upon **me**,*
*to shine on **me** as **I** dwell in darkness*
and the shadow of death,
*and to guide **my** feet into the way of peace.*

The Angels' Song:
The Gloria

Gloria in Excelsis

Glory to God in the highest,
and peace to God's people on earth.
Lord God, heavenly King,
almighty God and Father,
we worship you, we give you thanks,
we praise you for your glory.
Lord Jesus Christ, only Son of the Father,
Lord God, Lamb of God,
you take away the sin of the world:
have mercy on us;
you are seated at the right hand of the Father:
receive our prayer.
For you alone are the Holy One,
you alone are the Lord,
you alone are the Most High,
Jesus Christ,
with the Holy Spirit,
in the glory of God the Father. Amen.

Luke 2:13-14

*Suddenly a great company of the heavenly host appeared
with the angel, praising God and saying,
"Glory to God in the highest heaven,
    and on earth peace to those on whom
    his favour rests."*

Peace

Gloria in Excelsis

*Glory to God in the highest,
and peace to God's people on earth.*

Luke 2:13-14

*Suddenly a great company of the heavenly host appeared
with the angel, praising God and saying,
"Glory to God in the highest heaven,
and on earth peace to those on whom
his favour rests."*

Peace and good will. That's the message of Christmas. Hands up if you're against peace and good will… No one? Of course not! We're all in favour. Yet I suspect this talk of peace and good will contributes to giving Christianity a bad name. It sounds so soppy, so sentimental, so unrealistic, and therefore so irrelevant.

Two *thousand* years ago the angels said that Jesus would bring peace on earth. On the first Christmas Day, they sang, "Glory to God in the highest heaven, and on earth peace to those on whom his favour rests". You may know it better from the old King James Bible: "Glory to God in the highest, and on earth peace, good will toward men".

So, how's that going? It doesn't look good! The world is full of conflict and war. There are millions of refugees escaping poverty and violence. The news is full of stories of sexual harassment and violence against women.

Or come closer to home. I hope you'll have some peace and good will this Christmas. But if your family is typical, then chances are there will also be unspoken tensions, frayed tempers, slammed doors, uncomfortable silences. This Christmas there'll be families at war and people alone.

If Jesus came to bring peace and good will at that first Christmas, then 2,000 years on, he's clearly failed.

Peace and good will sounds like people saying, "Can't we just be nice to one another?" Imagine you're in a war zone. People have seen their homes destroyed, their daughters raped, their sons murdered, their families displaced. Your heart is torn apart. The wounds are deep. And someone says, "Could we perhaps try some peace and good will?" It's not real life.

Or maybe you know people who have written off Christianity because things are going well—a good job, money in the bank, a lovely home. Peace and good will sound good, but they're getting on fine without God. They don't see the need for the child in the manger.

We're going to see that the message of the angels is far more alarming than it first appears to be, but as a result, the peace it offers is far more real and relevant. For this is not simply a call to be nice to one another. What the angels sing is "peace *to* those on whom [God's] favour rests". This is not about peace *between* people. This is a peace that comes *from* God *to* humanity. It's a declaration that we can be at peace *with God*.

Human beings were made to find fulfilment and joy in God. Sometimes people say we have a "God-shaped hole" in our lives. That's kind of right, but it's not big enough to capture the reality. You can work round a hole. But God is our purpose and goal. No wonder we're restless without him. This is why everything else is ultimately a let-down—whether that's wealth or career or sex. While these things remain on the horizon, we can convince ourselves that we'll eventually reach them and when we do they'll eventually satisfy us. But if and when you arrive at your destination, you always find yourself wanting more. Doesn't your own life show this? You push to gain things, but when you get them, they don't satisfy in a lasting way. True peace is only found in God.

The Romans praised Emperor Caesar Augustus as the bringer of peace whose coming was good news. But it was a fragile peace, resting precariously on oppression and violence. It didn't address the restlessness within the human heart. In the same period that Luke wrote his Gospel, the stoic philosopher Epictetus (c. 50-130) wrote, "While the emperor may give peace from war on land and sea, he is unable to give peace from passion, grief, and envy. He cannot give peace of heart, for which man yearns more than even for outward peace."[12] Our hearts will always be restless until they find their rest in God through peace with God. This is the peace promised by the angels.

Yet when God comes to our world in the person of Jesus, he finds no home here. Luke tells us, "[Mary] wrapped him in cloths and placed him in a manger, because there was no guest room available for them" (v 7). Jesus exists outside of space; he made all space; and yet there's no space for him here on earth. Is there space for him in your life today? The fact that you're reading these words suggests there is! But don't let the busyness of life crowd him out as your day unfolds.

Reflection

All men are in search of happiness ... This is the motive for men's every action ... What does this greed and helplessness proclaim, except that there was once within us true happiness of which all that now remains is the outline and empty trace? Man tries unsuccessfully to fill this void with everything that surrounds him ... but ... this infinite abyss can be filled only with an infinite, immutable object, that is to say, God himself.[13]

Blaise Pascal
(1623-1662)

16

War

Luke 2:6-12

While they were there, the time came for the baby to be born, and she gave birth to her firstborn, a son. She wrapped him in cloths and placed him in a manger, because there was no guest room available for them.

And there were shepherds living out in the fields near by, keeping watch over their flocks at night. An angel of the Lord appeared to them, and the glory of the Lord shone around them, and they were terrified. But the angel said to them, "Do not be afraid. I bring you good news that will cause great joy for all the people. Today in the town of David a Saviour has been born to you; he is the Messiah, the Lord. This will be a sign to you: you will find a baby wrapped in cloths and lying in a manger."

If the angels' song celebrates a Saviour who will bring peace between God and humanity, then the alarming implication is that, without this Saviour, there's a war between God and humanity. Their song is actually very unnerving—it says that in ordinary life in this world *you* are at war with God.

It probably doesn't feel like that. You go to work, you watch TV, you hang out with friends—and all the time the thunderbolts are not falling. But make no mistake: each one of us has decided we don't want God in our lives. We've declared independence. We've ignored God. We've pushed him away. How do you think that's going to end? At the end of the day, on the final day, who do you think will win that war—you or God?

Let's come back to the angels' song, because the angels don't sing about the *beginning* of this war; they sing about its *end*. The lead angel says, "Do not be afraid. I bring you good news that will cause great joy for all the people" (v 10). To hear that you're at war with God is *not* good news. You'd have every reason to fear—were it not for Christmas. The message of the angel is that this bad news has turned into good news.

It's the good news of a Saviour. The angel continues, "Today ... a Saviour has been born to you" (v 11). The angel describes him as "the Messiah" (God's promised Saviour-King) and "the Lord" (the covenant God of Israel). What the shepherds actually get is a baby. The angel says, "This will be a sign to you: you will find a baby wrapped in cloths and lying in a manger" (v 12). But in verse 21, we're told that this baby is "named Jesus", and the word "Jesus" means "the Lord saves". Jesus comes to save.

Luke describes Jesus as Mary's "firstborn" in verse 7. It's an odd word to use. Why tell us this when we already know that Mary is a virgin? I think Luke wants us to see Mary's firstborn as none other than God's firstborn. Luke was good friends with the apostle Paul, and Paul wrote, "The Son is the image of the invisible God, the firstborn over all creation" (Colossians 1:15). It's not that the Father created Jesus at some point in time. No, the Son is *eternally* begotten of the Father. Jesus receives life from the Father from ever and for ever with no before or after. Augustine of Hippo says, "He was born of the Father always, of his mother once".[14] The point is that the Son is one being with the Father and the Spirit. He is God from God, coming to bring peace with God.

Talk of the "firstborn" also takes us back to the exodus, when God rescued his people from slavery. As we saw when we looked at the Benedictus, the final plague was the death of every firstborn child. God's people only escaped by sacrificing a lamb and daubing its blood round their door. The firstborn was the representative of the family, and the lamb died in the firstborn's place. Mary's firstborn is God's firstborn, the Passover lamb whom God sent to die in our place.

A few verses after calling Jesus "the firstborn over all creation", Paul writes, "Once you were alienated from God and were enemies in your minds because of your evil behaviour. But now [God] has reconciled you by Christ's physical body through death to present you holy in his sight" (Colossians 1:21-22). What was implicit in the song of the angels is here made explicit—Paul speaks of us as "alienated from God" and "enemies" of God. But these verses also come with an invitation to be "reconciled" to God.

No doubt you've received some invitations this Christmas—to family gatherings, work events or Christmas parties. But the real Christmas invitation is an invitation to come home to God, to enjoy peace with God. The angel tells the shepherds not simply that "a Saviour has been born" but that "a Saviour has been born *to you*" (Luke 2:11). On the first Christmas Day, in the town of David, a Saviour was born—to you.

Reflection

*See here what the gospel is, namely, a joyful sermon about Christ our Saviour ... What greater joy can anyone hear than that Christ is given **to me as my own**? The angel not only says that Christ is born, but he also makes Christ's birth **my own** by saying "**your** Saviour". The gospel not only teaches the history and events of Christ but also makes him **our own** and gives him to all who believe it ... What would it help me if Christ had been born a thousand times ... if I were never to hear that he was born for **me** and was to be **my very own?!*** [15]

Martin Luther
(1483–1546)

17

Seated

Gloria in Excelsis

Lord Jesus Christ, only Son of the Father,
Lord God, Lamb of God,
you take away the sin of the world:
have mercy on us;
you are seated at the right hand of the Father:
receive our prayer...

Christmas was supposed to bring peace between God and humanity. Did Jesus finish the job? The liturgical form of the angels' song is *Gloria in Excelsis*. This ancient hymn takes the angels' song from Luke 2 and expands it with other lines from the New Testament. We don't know who wrote it or when, but it was in regular use by the 4th century. Two of its lines show *how* Jesus has brought peace with God through his death on the cross.

1. The Lamb of God who takes away sin

The *Gloria* addresses Jesus as "Lamb of God", adding, "You take away the sin of the world". It's an allusion to John 1:29, where John the Baptist says, "Look, the Lamb of God, who takes away the sin of the world!" It's a picture drawn from the temple, where a lamb was a sacrifice for sin. There were different types of sacrifice—we'll focus on two. First, in the sin and guilt offerings, an animal (often a lamb) died in the place of the people (Leviticus 5 – 6). The lamb received the death their sins deserved so that they might walk free. Second, in the peace or fellowship offering, the fat of the lamb was offered to God as a "food offering" while the people ate the meat (3:1-17; 7:11-21). In effect, the people were eating a meal with God as a sign of restored peace. Add all these signs of the coming Lamb of God together and we see that Jesus died in our place as a sacrifice for our sin, to restore peace between us and God—a peace we celebrate when we eat the Communion meal with Jesus.

2. The seated Saviour whose work is done

After describing Jesus as the "Lamb of God", the *Gloria* says, "You are seated at the right hand of the Father". This line is an allusion to Hebrews 10:11-14:

> *Day after day every priest stands and performs his religious duties; again and again he offers the same sacrifices, which can never take away sins. But when this priest had offered for all time one sacrifice for sins, **he sat down at the right hand of God**, and since that time he waits for his enemies to be made his footstool. For by one sacrifice he has made perfect for ever those who are being made holy.*

Here, Jesus is not only the sacrifice; he's also the priest. He's our priest because he himself was the one who freely and willingly offered himself as the sacrifice.

What's that got to do with sitting down? The priests in the old temple had to keep on offering sacrifices because a dead lamb was never really going to deal with sin (Hebrews 10:1-4). Sacrifices were only a pointer to the real thing, and the real thing is Jesus. So after Jesus our priest had offered himself as our sacrifice, he sat down. Why? Because his work was done. Because his sacrifice was complete. He offered "for all time one sacrifice" because his death covered all the sins of all his people, now and for ever (v 12). Job done.

In medieval times, *Gloria in Excelsis* was used to introduce the reading of the Bible. But in the Book of Common Prayer, the great reforming Archbishop of Canterbury Thomas Cranmer moved it to the conclusion of the Communion service. Placing it there made it a reminder that the peace we enjoy with God is the result of the sacrifice we celebrate in communion.[16] We can only sing of peace with God because we have first partaken in the death of Christ. The manger is only the beginning of the story; the climax is the cross.

We declared war on God. And God sent an army; "a great company of the heavenly host" in Luke 2:13 is military language. But what does God's army do when it arrives? It declares peace!

Later in Luke's Gospel, a notoriously sinful woman gate-crashes a party to anoint the feet of Jesus. This scandalises the host. But Jesus says to the woman, "Your sins are forgiven … Your faith has saved you; go in peace" (7:48-50). Today, if you come to Jesus in faith, he says to you, *Your sins are forgiven. Go in peace for there is peace for God's people on earth.*

Reflection

The whole life of Christ was a continual passion; others die martyrs, but Christ was born a martyr. He found a Golgotha, where he was crucified, even in Bethlehem, where he was born; for to his tenderness then the straws were almost as sharp as the thorns after, and the manger as uneasy at first as his cross at last. His birth and his death were but one continual act, and his Christmas Day and his Good Friday are but the evening and morning of one and the same day.[17]

John Donne
(1572–1631)

18

Power

Luke 2:1-4

In those days Caesar Augustus issued a decree that a census should be taken of the entire Roman world. (This was the first census that took place while Quirinius was governor of Syria.) And everyone went to their own town to register. So Joseph also went up from the town of Nazareth in Galilee to Judea, to Bethlehem the town of David, because he belonged to the house and line of David.

Jesus has reconciled God and humanity. But what about peace on earth? Does Christianity have anything to say about the pain so many will experience this Christmas? It does. Indeed, politics and power were a big part of the first Christmas Day.

Everyone knows the action takes place in Bethlehem. But why Bethlehem? Luke gives us two reasons. First, Mary and Joseph go to Bethlehem because Caesar Augustus has ordered a census which requires people to register in their home town (v 1-3). It's an act of imperial power. A decree is made in Rome, and hundreds of miles away a young peasant woman is forced to make a long journey in the final days of her pregnancy. In Matthew's account of the Nativity, King Herod (the local puppet king) massacres the baby boys of Bethlehem, and Jesus only escapes by becoming a refugee (Matthew 2:13-16). We can't ignore the politics of the world—not even in our Nativity plays. This is a story about invading armies, onerous taxation and forced migration.

But there's a second reason why Jesus was born in Bethlehem. Luke says Mary and Joseph go to Bethlehem so that Jesus can be born in "the town of David" (Luke 2:4). David was Israel's greatest king, and this is a big hint that Jesus would be David's successor—the ultimate Saviour-King who would liberate God's people and restore God's reign (Micah 5:1-2; 2 Samuel 7:12-16).

Remember Mary's song—there's plenty of politics there too! "He has brought down rulers from their thrones," she sings, "but has lifted up the humble" (Luke 1:52). There are many parts of the world where these words could get you arrested.

A day is coming when Jesus will turn the world upside down, and we get a glimpse of that on the first Christmas Day. As God's King is coming into our world, angels appear to shepherds who become the first people to hear the "good news". Yet shepherds were low-status people; it was a job for ne'er-do-wells. God is bringing down rulers and lifting up the humble—just as Mary said he would do.

What about now? We're living in an in-between time—between the first coming of Jesus, when he gave us a glimpse of God's kingdom, and the second coming of Jesus, when he will establish God's kingdom for ever. In between these two comings, Jesus is giving people an opportunity to repent. He's offering a peace deal. One day Jesus will come to right every wrong, but first he offers forgiveness to any who will turn to him in faith. The delay is not a sign of apathy or weakness; it's a sign of divine patience. Jesus is like a judge offering a pardon before he passes sentence, or a police chief offering an amnesty before making arrests, or an army general offering a peace treaty before battle commences.

A day is coming when the last bullet will be fired, when the last girl will be sold into prostitution, when the last elderly woman will be conned out of her savings, when the last person will be abused because of their skin colour. A day of reckoning is coming when evil will be exposed and judgment will be passed. A new day will dawn, and there will be peace on earth.

In the meantime, Luke's Gospel ends with Jesus declaring, "Repentance for the forgiveness of sins will be preached in [my] name to all nations" (Luke 24:47). Today that message reaches you. Bring your wrongdoing to him today and you will be forgiven—perhaps for the first time, perhaps for the hundredth time. Bring your restlessness to him today and find peace.

Reflection

Hark, the glad sound, the Saviour comes,
The Saviour promised long!
Let every heart prepare a throne,
And every voice a song.

He comes the prisoners to release,
In Satan's bondage held;
The gates of brass before him burst,
The iron fetters yield.

He comes the broken heart to bind,
The bleeding soul to cure,
And with the riches of his grace,
To enrich the humbled poor.

Our glad hosannas, Prince of Peace,
Thy welcome shall proclaim;
And heaven's eternal arches ring
With thy beloved Name.

From "Hark the Glad Sound"
Philip Doddridge
(1702–1751)

19

Glory

Gloria in Excelsis

*Glory to God in the highest,
and peace to God's people on earth.*

Luke 2:15-20

When the angels had left them and gone into heaven, the shepherds said to one another, "Let's go to Bethlehem and see this thing that has happened, which the Lord has told us about." So they hurried off and found Mary and Joseph, and the baby, who was lying in the manger. When they had seen him, they spread the word concerning what had been told them about this child, and all who heard it were amazed at what the shepherds said to them. But Mary treasured up all these things and pondered them in her heart. The shepherds returned, glorifying and praising God for all the things they had heard and seen, which were just as they had been told.

So far, we've focused on the second half of the angels' song. We've looked at the message of peace on earth to those on whom God's favour rests. But the song begins, "Glory to God in the highest" (v 14). It's the anthem of those who rejoice in God's peace.

The two lines of the song parallel one another:

Glory	in the highest heaven	to God.
Peace	on earth	to those on whom his favour rests.

As peace comes to God's people on earth, glory rises to God in heaven. Our role is to complete that process—to respond to God's gift of peace with our songs of praise. God comes to us in Christ, and in Christ we come to God.

The Puritan Isaac Ambrose says the incarnation is the greatest ever miracle. "It is a great mystery, a secret, a wonder. There have been many wonders since the beginning of the world, but all the wonders that ever were must give pride of place to the incarnation, compared to which they cease to be wonderful!"[18] The Creator becoming a creature while remaining the Creator is more amazing even than the creation of the whole vast universe out of nothing. It should take our breath away, and then, when we recover our breath, it should make us sing!

Writing about the prophecies of the Old Testament, Peter says, "Even angels long to look into these things" (1 Peter 1:12). It's impossible for us to think our way into the mind of an angel. Did they struggle to grasp what the prophets were saying? Did they struggle to see how all the strands of God's promises would come together? We don't know. But when those strands did fall into place on the first Christmas Day, they broke into song. It was a song of heaven that reverberated down to earth. They couldn't contain their excitement and wonder. It burst out of heaven and showered down in bright sparkles to the cold, dark skies over Bethlehem's fields.

But the angels' song was not the only song to be sung in the fields of Bethlehem that night. After they had seen Jesus in the manger, we read, "The shepherds returned, glorifying and praising God for all the things they had heard and seen, which were just as they had been told" (Luke 2:20). What do the shepherds do when they see what God has done? They sing, "Glory to God in the highest". They join the song of the angels.

When the shepherds first saw the angel, "they were terrified" (v 9). It's literally "they were afraid with great fear". That's the natural reaction of rebellious human beings when they encounter members of God's angelic army! But the angel offers them "great joy" (v 10). Their "great fear" can become "great joy". And that's exactly what *does* happen when they see the Saviour. Once you see what God has done in sending his Son, you'll want to glorify God. The 17th-century Puritan Richard Sibbes says, "The angels begin with the main and chief end of all. It is God's end; it was the angels' end, and it should be ours too … The glory of God, the setting forth of the excellencies and eminences of the Lord, should be the end of our lives, the chief thing we should aim at."[19]

This is your cue. The conductor is waving the baton in your direction. Peace has reached you through the coming of Jesus, and that means it's time to sing.

Reflection

Heaven and earth are united today, for Christ is born!
Today God has come upon earth,
and humankind gone up to heaven.
Today, for the sake of humankind,
the invisible one is seen in the flesh.
Therefore let us glorify him and cry aloud:
glory to God in the highest,
and on earth peace bestowed by your coming,
Saviour: glory to you!
Today in Bethlehem, I hear the angels:
Glory to God in the highest!
Glory to him whose good pleasure it was
that there be peace on earth!
The Virgin is now more spacious than the heavens.
Light has shone on those in darkness,
exalting the lowly who sing like the angels:
Glory to God in the highest![20]

John the Monk
(c. 650–750)

Simeon's Song:
The Nunc Dimittis

Now, Lord, you let your servant go in peace:
your word has been fulfilled.

My own eyes have seen the salvation
which you have prepared in the sight of every people;

A light to reveal you to the nations
and the glory of your people Israel.

Luke 2:25-35

[25] Now there was a man in Jerusalem called Simeon, who was righteous and devout. He was waiting for the consolation of Israel, and the Holy Spirit was on him. [26] It had been revealed to him by the Holy Spirit that he would not die before he had seen the Lord's Messiah. [27] Moved by the Spirit, he went into the temple courts. When the parents brought in the child Jesus to do for him what the custom of the Law required, [28] Simeon took him in his arms and praised God, saying:

[29] "Sovereign Lord, as you have promised,
    you may now dismiss your servant in peace.
[30] For my eyes have seen your salvation,

³¹ which you have prepared in the sight of all nations:
³² a light for revelation to the Gentiles,
and the glory of your people Israel."

³³ The child's father and mother marvelled at what was said about him. ³⁴ Then Simeon blessed them and said to Mary, his mother: "This child is destined to cause the falling and rising of many in Israel, and to be a sign that will be spoken against, ³⁵ so that the thoughts of many hearts will be revealed. And a sword will pierce your own soul too."

20

Waiting

Nunc Dimittis

Now, Lord, you let your servant go in peace:
your word has been fulfilled.

Luke 2:25-29

Now there was a man in Jerusalem called Simeon,
who was righteous and devout. He was waiting for the
consolation of Israel, and the Holy Spirit was on him.
It had been revealed to him by the Holy Spirit that he
would not die before he had seen the Lord's Messiah.
Moved by the Spirit, he went into the temple courts.
When the parents brought in the child Jesus to do for
him what the custom of the Law required, Simeon took
him in his arms and praised God, saying:

"Sovereign Lord, as you have promised,
  you may now dismiss your servant in peace."

How are you at waiting? Do you hop from foot to foot as you wait in line, muttering about the time, ever alert for queue jumpers?

We know very little about Simeon. But what we do know is that he was "righteous and devout" (v 25). What does a righteous and devout believer do all day? Luke says Simeon "was waiting" (v 25).

Luke uses a similar expression to describe another "righteous" man (23:50, ESV)—Joseph of Arimathea, the man who buried Jesus. Luke introduces Joseph by saying he "was *waiting* for the kingdom of God" (v 51). So Luke begins and ends his Gospel with two righteous, waiting men; Jesus is lovingly welcomed into this world by waiting Simeon, and he's lovingly buried by waiting Joseph.

Simeon is waiting for "the consolation of Israel". The Holy Spirit had told Simeon "he would not die before he had seen the Lord's Messiah" (2:26). So he waits for Israel's promised comfort through the coming of the Messiah (Isaiah 40:1). God's people were in exile because of God's judgment on their sin. But a day would come when the penalty of Israel's sin would be paid and God himself would tend "his flock like a shepherd" (v 2, 11). That's the day of comfort or consolation for which Simeon waits (52:9).

Then one morning, perhaps as Simeon was praying, the Holy Spirit moved him to go to the temple (Luke 2:27). Imagine how Simeon felt as he made his way through the streets of Jerusalem. Was this the day? Was his long wait about to end?

Simeon's story is shaped like an X with its different moments paralleling one another around a central point in an arrangement known as a "chiasm" (after the Greek letter Χ or "chi"):

  A. Simeon is waiting for the consolation of Israel.
    B. Simeon is told he will not die until he has seen it.
      C. Simeon holds Jesus in his arms.
    B'. Simeon says he can die because now he has seen it.
  A'. Simeon has seen the glory of Israel.

Setting it out like this shows how the anticipation builds until the central moment, and this is then followed by a release of tension as Simeon's hopes are realised and he holds Jesus in his arms (v 27-28).

Jesus is still only a few weeks old. This is not an army poised to overthrow the Romans. This is not a host of angels ready to take on evil. This is not an intellectual movement bringing enlightenment. God's solution to all the problems of the world is a baby.

But what a baby! The Comfort of God is nestled in Simeon arms! God himself has come to shepherd his people; all the power of deity is squeezed into a fragile human body. This is Simeon's Saviour-King and his redeeming Lord. Imagine how he felt as he looked into the face of "the child Jesus".

Simeon's wait is over because Jesus the Messiah has come. Simeon describes himself as God's "servant" (v 29). Picture a servant who's been commanded to carry an important delivery to its destination or protect an important person on a journey. All the time they feel the weight of their responsibility. So when that responsibility is finally discharged, there's a sense of relief. As Simeon holds Jesus in his arms, the burden of waiting is over, and he's finally released from the responsibility he has borne.

"Let your servant go in peace" is his way of saying, *Relieve me of my duties because my task is complete.* The Messiah has come, and Simeon is consoled.

But Jesus is also coming again. The word "advent" means "coming", and in the advent season we not only look to Christ's coming at Christmas, but we also and primarily look forward to his coming in glory. We, too, are waiting for our consolation. Paul describes the Thessalonian Christians as "model" believers, like "righteous" Simeon. And what do model believers do all day? They wait, like Simeon. Paul says they have turned from idols to serve God "and *to wait* for his Son from heaven" (1 Thessalonians 1:7-10; see also Romans 8:23-25).

The wait for Jesus is over, and the wait for Jesus continues. Jesus has both come and is coming. He has come and redeemed us from sin, and he's coming again to make all things new. And those who are "righteous and devout" wait for his coming. The Bible ends with Jesus saying, "Yes, I am coming soon". To which we respond, "Amen. Come, Lord Jesus" (Revelation 22:20).

Reflection

I am waiting for the dawning
Of that bright and blessed day,
When the darksome night of sorrow
Shall have vanished far away;
When for ever with the Saviour,
Far beyond this vale of tears,
I shall swell the hymn of worship
Through the everlasting years.

I am waiting for the coming
Of the Lord, who died for me.
Oh, his words have thrilled my spirit,
"I will come again for thee."
I can almost hear his footfall
On the threshold of the door,
And my heart, my heart is longing
To be his for evermore.

S. Trevor Francis
(1834-1925)

21

Sleeping

Nunc Dimittis

Now, Lord, you let your servant go in peace:
your word has been fulfilled.

My own eyes have seen the salvation
which you have prepared in the sight of every people.

Luke 2:30-31

"Sovereign Lord, as you have promised,
 you may now dismiss your servant in peace.
For my eyes have seen your salvation,
 which you have prepared in the sight of all nations."

Imagine you have a condition that means you regularly fall unconscious. In those moments you are completely vulnerable. You are unable to protect yourself. And you can be out for several hours at a time. As you may have spotted, you *do* have such a condition; it's called "sleep".

Every day of our lives, our need to sleep reminds us of our limitations. Perhaps you can pull an "all-nighter" every now and then. But sooner or later you'll run out of steam and need to recharge. And while you do so, you're vulnerable. The world is a dangerous place, and our ability to protect ourselves is limited.

Sleep itself is not without its fears. I have a recurring nightmare in which I'm running from someone—I'm never caught, but I can never escape being pursued. The chase only ever ends with me waking up in a sweat. I wonder how often you have nightmares.

Simeon's song, the *Nunc Dimittis,* is traditionally sung as part of compline or night prayer. It's part of the way Christians over the centuries have prepared for bed. Of course, Simeon isn't getting ready for bed when he sings. When he says, "You may now dismiss your servant", he's getting ready for *death*. He's basically saying, *I'm now ready to die for I can meet death in peace.*

Simeon was told that "he would not die before he had seen the Lord's Messiah" (v 26). It's literally "he would not *see* death". Simeon would not *see* death until he had *seen* the Messiah. And when he does, he says, "My eyes have *seen* your salvation" (v 30). In the baby, he sees the Messiah, and in the Messiah, he sees salvation—he sees the Saviour.

The first word of Simeon's song in the original Greek is an emphatic "Now": *now, at last—now, because of this child—you can dismiss your servant in peace as you promised.* Simeon is not afraid of death. He dies happy because he's seen the salvation of God in the person of Jesus. Simeon could face death in peace because Jesus had come to conquer death.

There's much that Simeon wouldn't see. He probably didn't live to see Jesus preaching or performing miracles, and it's even less likely that he saw Jesus die or rise again. He didn't live to see the Holy Spirit poured out at Pentecost or the gospel being preached in all nations. But he did see Jesus, and that was enough.

Today most of us go to bed assuming we'll wake up the next morning. But previous generations couldn't think like that—preparing for bed was a kind of preparing for death. Indeed, in the Bible "sleep" is often used as a picture of death. Jesus said Jairus's daughter wasn't dead but asleep, before raising her back to life just as easily as you or I might rouse someone from sleep (8:52-55). Paul describes Christians who have died as "those who have fallen asleep" (1 Thessalonians 4:14-15). So in the past, people went to bed with a sense that, while they might awake in the same room, they might also awake in the presence of Christ. People felt the fragility of life. Even today, though we live longer on average, the death rate remains 100 percent!

But tonight, you can go to bed without fear. We don't have to fear the phantoms of the night because our King has come, and our King is bigger than our fears. Jesus has conquered death, and so the grave has become a bed, a place of sleep from which we rise. Night by night as we prepare for sleep we can say, "Now, Lord, you let your servant go in peace ... My own eyes have seen the salvation."

If you think your *identity* depends on you, then you can't go to bed in peace. You've got to prove yourself, and there are never enough hours in the day to pull that off. Or if you think your *future* depends on you, then you'll stay up to get things done, and still you won't have covered everything.

If this is what's keeping you awake, then you need to take your eyes off yourself and look to your Saviour. You may not have held Jesus in your arms as Simeon did, but you can see him with the eyes of faith in the gospel message (2 Corinthians 4:4-6). You can let your Saviour's grace dismiss you in peace—you have nothing to prove. And you can let your Saviour's care dismiss you in peace—tonight he has everything covered.

We can go to bed in peace, leaving our unfinished tasks in God's hands, leaving the care of those we love in God's hands, leaving our lives—and our deaths—in God's hands. We can go to bed in peace because we've seen God's salvation in the gospel of Christ.

Reflection

Simeon's heart became young again ... Therefore he sings this happy song of praise: "I will die now with joy in my heart, and death will seem sweet to me, for my eyes have seen your Saviour." That is the treasure that makes death sweet and dear. Whoever can see and recognize this young Lord who became subject to the law for us, his heart will be made happy against all adversity. See what kind of heart this venerable man had: "I am ready to depart in peace." It is a great word that he speaks: he will be happy and die in peace. Take a look at how people usually die: there is no joy in their hearts, but the heart beats and throbs, the body shakes and trembles, the mind goes blank. Death is too powerful ... But this man gives praise that he now can die as if there were no death. He doesn't even say "death," but "let [me] depart." He calls it a gentle departure. How can I learn to see death as a sweet sleep, when it is usually so terrifying? In this case, the law, sin and Satan were all removed from his heart.[21]

Martin Luther
(1483-1546)

22

Prepared

Nunc Dimittis

*My own eyes have seen the salvation
which you have prepared in the sight of every people.*

Luke 2:30-31

*For my eyes have seen your salvation,
    which you have prepared in the sight of all nations.*

My wife once started knitting a blanket for a friend's first child. My wife's not an accomplished knitter (though she's considerably more accomplished than me), and she ended up being distracted by other things. So when the blanket was given to her friend, it was given for her second child! The blanket turned out to be longer in the making than expected.

Simeon has been waiting all his life for the moment when he holds Jesus in his arms. But Simeon recognises that God's salvation plan has been a far longer time in the making. God wasn't simply responding on the hoof as events unfolded, nor was his plan thrown together at the last minute. Salvation has been carefully "prepared" by God.

That preparation, says Simeon, has taken place "in the sight of every people". Israel was God's showcase. It was as if God implanted a little enclave of light into the darkness of the rebellious world. Israel's life was to embody the holiness of God's character. Her laws were to model the goodness of his rule. Her institutions were to picture the grace of his salvation. Every sacrificial lamb pointed forward to God's coming salvation. Every prophet, priest and king pointed forward to God's Messiah—their successes were a picture of his work while their failures showed how much we needed Jesus. Every victory pointed forward to the victory of Jesus at the cross.

Why the wait? Why not send Jesus immediately after Adam's fall? Perhaps it's because we need the history of Israel to show us who Jesus is and what he accomplishes. Without the Old Testament, we can't grasp the full meaning of Christ's coming. This is why Luke, even though he's writing to Gentiles, starts his Gospel with these four songs steeped in the Old Testament. Simeon says (as the Nunc Dimittis puts it), "Now, Lord, you let your servant go in peace: your word has been fulfilled." That may be a reference to the promise he received from the Spirit that he wouldn't see death until he had seen the Saviour (v 26). But its meaning goes far beyond that, to encompass every word of the Old Testament.

At the end of Luke's Gospel, the risen Christ meets confused and frightened disciples on the road to Emmaus. Failing to recognise Jesus, they tell him how all their hopes have been dashed. "We had hoped that he was the one who was going to redeem Israel," they say (Luke 24:20). Just like Simeon, they're waiting for the consolation of Israel. But by this point it's happened, and they have missed it! So Jesus says to them, "How foolish you are, and how slow to believe all that the prophets have spoken! Did not the Messiah have to suffer these things and then enter his glory?" (v 25-26). Then Luke tells us, "Beginning with Moses and all the Prophets, he explained to them what was said in all the Scriptures concerning himself" (v 27). What a Bible study that was! Jesus is the fulfilment of "all the Scriptures". That's what Simeon realised, even though he was only holding a tiny baby.

But in fact, God's preparations go further back beyond Israel—back to the origins of humanity and the promise to Adam that one of Eve's offspring would crush the serpent. And they go back still further, before the very beginnings of time. From all eternity, the triune God has agreed this plan of salvation with the incarnation at its centre. Theologians speak of "the covenant of redemption": an eternal agreement between Father, Son and Spirit to redeem a people who will be Christ's people. It's not that God created a world and then, when things turned ugly, he had to come up with a remedy. Instead, God planned a dramatic demonstration of his love in Christ, created a world and gave it a history, all to be the stage upon which this act of love would be performed. The universe is a theatre set for the cross of Christ.

It's not just Simeon's wait which is over. Israel's wait is over. Creation's wait is over. Love's wait is over. History and eternity all converge on the child in Simeon's arms.

Reflection

What greater distance can there be than between Deity and humanity, between the Creator and a creature? Can you imagine the distance between eternity and time, infinite power and miserable infirmity, an immortal Spirit and dying flesh, the highest being and nothing? Yet these are married in the person of Christ. A God of unmixed blessedness is linked personally with a man of perpetual sorrows, life incapable of death joined to a body destined to die, almightiness and weakness, omniscience and ignorance, immutability and changeableness, that which cannot be comprehended and that which can be comprehended, that which is entirely independent and that which is totally dependent, the Creator forming all things and the creature he made—all meet together in a personal union, the Word made flesh (John 1:14), the eternal Son and the seed of Abraham (Hebrews 2:16). What is more miraculous than for God to become man and man to become God! Nothing less than an incomprehensible power could bring about this plan of incomprehensible wisdom.[22]

Stephen Charnock
(1628–1680)

23

Exposed

Luke 2:34-35

Then Simeon blessed them and said to Mary, his mother: "This child is destined to cause the falling and rising of many in Israel, and to be a sign that will be spoken against, so that the thoughts of many hearts will be revealed. And a sword will pierce your own soul too."

Simeon holds in his arms a sign from God in human form. It's wonderful! But what does this mean for our towns and neighbourhoods? We need to connect these high thoughts to our everyday lives. And in our everyday lives most people are not interested in Jesus. They don't see him as a vision of divine glory.

That's because not only does Jesus reveal God's glory; Jesus also reveals our hearts. He exposes our true colours. Jesus is a sign—a sign of God's glory. But he's a sign that will be spoken *against*. Not everyone will greet this sign as Simeon did.

It doesn't take long. Jesus starts his ministry by preaching in his home town and his neighbours try to push him off a cliff (Luke 4:28-29). The religious people denounce him. The Jewish leaders accuse him before Pilate. The crowd shouts, "Crucify him". Pilate announces his death sentence. Throughout his life people speak against Jesus until, in the end, those words turn to violence. That's why Simeon warns Mary, "A sword will pierce your own soul too" (2:35). Mary is going to see her son crucified.

And still today, Jesus is a sign that is spoken *against*. In your workplace, on your television set, on your social-media feed, people speak against Jesus because he reveals our hearts. Our attitude to God is revealed in our attitude to his Son. Why don't people accept Jesus? Because we're proud or self-willed or both. That's what's exposed by an encounter with Jesus. We think we can manage without God, and we resist his involvement in our lives.

Simeon says, "This child is destined to cause the falling and rising of many" (v 34). In other words, Jesus brings salvation and judgment. Some people hear the message of Jesus, put their trust in him and receive eternal life. Other people hear the *same* message, reject Jesus and are condemned. Jesus himself will say:

> *Do you think I came to bring peace on earth? No, I tell you, but division. From now on there will be five in one family divided against each other, three against two and two against three. They will be divided, father against son and son against father, mother against daughter and daughter against mother, mother-in-law against daughter-in-law and daughter-in-law against mother-in-law. (12:51-53)*

Right now, your heart is being revealed. You hear the story of Simeon holding Jesus in his arms. You hear the words, "A light of revelation to the nations". Perhaps your heart rises in excitement, joy and wonder. Or perhaps your heart sinks in fear or anger or simply boredom. Either your heart rises to embrace Jesus with faith or your heart moves on to other thoughts, other hopes, other dreams. This will be the basis on which you are judged. Even as these words are read, Jesus is causing the rising or the falling of those who hear this message.

How do you respond this Christmas to Immanuel, God with us?

Reflection

Sacred Infant, all divine,
What a tender love was thine,
Thus to come from highest bliss,
Down to such a world as this.

Teach, O teach us, holy Child,
By thy face so meek and mild,
Teach us to resemble thee,
In thy sweet humility.

from "See, Amid the Winter's Snow"
Edward Caswall
(1814-1878)

24

Rewarded

Nunc Dimittis

*A light to reveal you to the nations
and the glory of your people Israel.*

Luke 2:32

*A light for revelation to the Gentiles,
    and the glory of your people Israel.*

Simeon's short song is packed full of echoes of the prophet Isaiah. To make sense of it, we need to go to Isaiah 49:3-6:

*He said to me, "You are my servant,
    Israel, in whom I will display my splendour."
But I said, "I have laboured in vain;
    I have spent my strength for nothing at all.
Yet what is due me is in the LORD's hand,*

> *and my reward is with my God."*
> *And now the LORD says—*
> *he who formed me in the womb to be his servant*
> *to bring Jacob back to him*
> *and gather Israel to himself,*
> *for I am honoured in the eyes of the LORD*
> *and my God has been my strength—*
> *he says: "It is too small a thing for you to be my servant*
> *to restore the tribes of Jacob*
> *and bring back those of Israel I have kept.*
> *I will also make you a light for the Gentiles,*
> *that my salvation may reach to the ends of the earth."*

In the first instance, God's servant is the nation of Israel. That's clear from verse 3, where the servant is named as "Israel". Israel was called to be a light to the nations. God called to her to "display my splendour". As his people lived under God's rule expressed in his law, they would show the nations that God is good and his rule is good. Isaiah 60:3 says, "Nations will come to your light, and kings to the brightness of your dawn." But the Israelites didn't live under God's rule, and they didn't obey his law. Indeed, they damaged God's reputation. That's why they ended up in exile. Israel was judged because "God's name is blasphemed among the Gentiles because of you" (Romans 2:24; Isaiah 52:5). Israel was supposed to be a light to the nations. But in fact, Israel herself needed rescuing, gathering, comforting, redeeming.

So, through Isaiah, God promises a *new* servant. And Simeon's echoes of Isaiah are his way of saying the baby in his arms is going to be this servant promised by Isaiah. What will Jesus the Servant do?

First, Jesus will restore faithful Israel. In Isaiah 49:5 the new servant says God formed him to "gather Israel to himself". Imagine a breakdown truck on its way to rescue a stranded car. Only this breakdown truck is not fit for purpose. Before long, it too breaks down. It too needs to be rescued. Israel was given the job of rescuing the nations, but she wasn't fit for purpose. So God sends out another rescue vehicle. "My God has been my strength," says verse 5. This is the souped-up Rolls Royce of breakdown trucks! This is Jesus, the Son of God empowered by the Spirit of God. He comes as the "consolation of Israel" and "the glory of your people Israel" (Luke 2:25, 32). Believing Jews find forgiveness and restoration in Jesus.

But the mission of Jesus reaches beyond the confines of Judaism. Riffing off of Isaiah, Simeon says Jesus is "a light to reveal [God] to the nations". Israel failed to display God's splendour; she failed to be God's glory in human form. But now here is Jesus, the glory of God, in Simeon's arms. Luke's account of Jesus' life in his Gospel is full of that glory, and some of it spills over onto Gentiles (such as the Roman centurion whose servant is healed by Jesus in Luke 7:1-10). Ultimately, the Gospel will end with Jesus commissioning his disciples to proclaim "the forgiveness of sins … in his name to all nations" (24:47).

In Isaiah 49:4 the Servant says, "I have laboured in vain; I have spent my strength for nothing at all". Imagine Jesus as he is dying on the cross. It looks as if his life has ended in failure. But then the Father speaks: "It is too small a thing for you to be my servant to restore the tribes of Jacob and bring back those of Israel I have kept" (v 6). Restoring Israel is not enough. The cross deserves more; the salvation of Jesus is going to "reach to the ends of the earth" (v 6).

This is where you come in. You have heard the story of salvation. Today, as you read these words, "a light for revelation" is shining upon you. You are the proof that God's "word has been fulfilled". If you're a Christian, you are Christ's reward.

Reflection

I cannot tell how silently he suffered,
As with his peace he graced this place of tears,
Or how his heart upon the cross was broken,
The crown of pain to three and thirty years ...
But this I know, all flesh shall see his glory,
And he shall reap the harvest he has sown,
And some glad day his sun shall shine in splendour
When he the Saviour, Saviour of the world is known.

from "I Cannot Tell Why He, Whom Angels Worship"
William Young Fullerton
(1857-1932)

Endnotes

1. Robert C. Tannehill, *The Narrative Unity of Luke-Acts: A Literary Interpretation, Volume One: The Gospel According to Luke* (Fortress Press, 1986), p. 17-19.

2. Michael Ramsey, *The Christian Priest Today* (SPCK, Rev. Ed., 1985), p. 42.

3. C.H. Spurgeon, Sermon No. 3019, "The Hungry Filled, The Rich Emptied," (Luke 1:53).

4. Adapted from Martin Luther, "Afternoon Sermon on the Visitation" (1535); cited in Beth Kreitzer (ed.), *Luke,* Reformation Commentary on Scripture: New Testament Volume III (IVP Academic, 2015), p. 27.

5. Stephen Charnock, *The Existence and Attributes of God, Volume 1*, ed. Mark Jones (Crossway, 2022), p. 971.

6. Richard B. Hays, *Echoes of Scripture in the Gospels* (Baylor University Press, 2016), p. 271.

7. "O Holy Night" was written by the French poet Placide Cappeau (1808–1877) and translated by the Unitarian John Sullivan Dwight (1813–1893).

8. C.H. Spurgeon, Sermon No. 1907, "The Tender

Mercy of Our God (Luke 1:77-79)", in *C.H. Spurgeon, The Treasury of the Bible: The New Testament Volume 1* (Marshall, Morgan and Scott, 1962), p. 616.

9   Ambrose, *Exposition of the Gospel of Luke 2.41-42.26*; cited in Arthur A. Just Jr (ed.), *Luke,* Ancient Christian Commentary on Scripture: Volume 3 (Intervarsity Press, 2003), p. 38.

10   Heinrich Bullinger; cited in Beth Kreitza (ed.), *Luke,* Reformation Commentary on Scripture: New Testament Volume III (IVP Academic, 2015), p. 43.

11   C.H. Spurgeon, Sermon No. 1907, "The First Christmas Carol (Luke 2:14)", in *C.H. Spurgeon, The Treasury of the Bible: The New Testament Volume 1* (Marshall, Morgan and Scott, 1962), p. 639-640.

12   Epictetus; quoted in Daniel M. Doriani, Philip Graham Ryken, and Richard D. Philips, *The Incarnation in the Gospels,* Reformed Expository Commentary (P&R, 2008), p. 111.

13   Blaise Pascal, *Pensées and Other Writings*, trans. Honor Levi (OUP, 1995), XI.181, p. 51-52.

14   Augustine, "Sermon 372.1"; cited in Arthur A. Just Jr (ed.), *Luke,* Ancient Christian Commentary on Scripture: Volume 3 (Intervarsity Press, 2003), p. 41.

15   Adapted from Martin Luther, "The Church Postil (1540): Christmas Day"; cited in Beth Kreitza (ed.), *Luke,* Reformation Commentary on Scripture: New

Testament Volume III (IVP Academic, 2015), p. 51. Emphasis added.

16 Common Worship (the Church of England's library of liturgical resources introduced in 2000) has moved it back to its medieval location before the reading of the word in the Communion service.

17 John Donne, "Sermon 4, Preached at Saint Paul's on Christmas Day (1626)"; cited in Beth Kreitza (ed.), *Luke,* Reformation Commentary on Scripture: New Testament Volume III (IVP Academic, 2015), p. 49.

18 Adapted from Isaac Ambrose, *Looking Unto Jesus* (1658), Sprinkle Publications, 1986, p. 175.

19 Richard Sibbes, *The Complete Works, Volume 6,* ed. Alexander Balloch Grosart (Banner of Truth, 1973), p. 322, 324.

20 John the Monk, *Stichera of the Nativity of the Lord*; cited in Arthur A. Just Jr (ed.), *Luke,* Ancient Christian Commentary on Scripture: Volume 3 (Intervarsity Press, 2003), p. 41-42.

21 Martin Luther, "A Sermon from February 2, 1526"; cited in Beth Kreitza (ed.), *Luke,* Reformation Commentary on Scripture: New Testament Volume III (IVP Academic, 2015), p. 61.

22 Abridged and adapted from Stephen Charnock, *The Existence and Attributes of God, Volume 1*, ed. Mark Jones (Crossway, 2022), p. 974-975.

BIBLICAL | RELEVANT | ACCESSIBLE

At The Good Book Company we are dedicated to helping Christians and local churches grow. We believe that God's growth process always starts with hearing clearly what he has said to us through his timeless and flawless word—the Bible.

Ever since we opened our doors in 1991, we have been striving to produce resources that are biblical, relevant, and accessible. By God's grace, we have grown to become an international publisher, encouraging ordinary Christians of every age and stage and every background and denomination to live for Christ day by day and equipping churches to grow in their knowledge of God, their love for one another, and the effectiveness of their outreach.

Call one of our friendly team for a discussion of your needs or visit one of our local websites for more information on the resources and services we provide.

Your friends at The Good Book Company

thegoodbook.com | thegoodbook.co.uk
thegoodbook.com.au | thegoodbook.co.nz